ORTHODOX CHRISTIAN SOCIAL THOUGHT

The Cure for Consumerism

Fr. Gregory Jensen

Edited by Dylan Pahman

ACTONINSTITUTE

Orthodox Christian Social Thought Series, Number 2

Cover image: A colorful collage made up of newspaper clippings and sales papers on the topic of "BLACK FRIDAY"
Contributor: Allkindza
Source: ©iStock.com

ISBN: 978-1-942503-01-9

ACTONINSTITUTE

98 E. Fulton
Grand Rapids, Michigan 49503
Phone: 616.454.3080
Fax: 616.454.9454
www.acton.org

Cover design by Peter Ho
Copy edited by Jan M. Ortiz
Interior composition by Judy Schafer

Printed in the United States of America

Contents

1 Introduction

Consumerism and the Ascetical Life

Judging Wisely

There is a story told about two monks—one a former Roman imperial official, the other an elder herdsman from Egypt—who both "resided at Scete."[1] The desert fathers of ancient Egypt were known for leading rigorous ascetical lives of prayer, fasting, and manual labor in their pursuit of Christian holiness. Therefore it came as quite a surprise to the former herdsman to see his brother monk "clothed in soft garments" (see Luke 7:25) and sleeping on "a mat with fleece on it … and a small pillow." In addition to these things the Roman had clean feet, wore sandals, and "for his weakness … had a little wine"! The Egyptian is scandalized that his brother monk is "living in such luxury rather than in austerity," and he goes away "unenlightened."[2]

---

1 The story can be found in John Wortley, trans., *Book of the Elders* (Collegeville, MN: Cistercian Publications, 2012), 170–72. The term *scete* (more commonly, skete) refers to a small monastic community. For more on the history of this term, see *The Coptic Encyclopedia*, s.v. "Scete," http://ccdl.libraries.claremont.edu/cdm/ref/collection/cce/id/1715.

2 Wortley, *Book of the Elders*, 171–72.

However, as the story goes, after the Egyptian "had gone a little way," the first monk "called him back, receiving him joyfully when he returned." The elder then begins to ask his brother about his life before he came to the monastery. Here is where we find out that, unlike the elder, he is not a Roman citizen but a village herdsman who often slept outside on the cold, hard ground. His meals were scant and simple; he would eat "a little bread with salted fish and drink water." Because his village had no bathhouse, like the rest of the villagers, he "would wash … in the river."

Hearing all this, the elder declares that his brother's life before coming to the monastery was one of "severe hardship." His own life before coming to the monastery, however, was much different. He owned "great houses and much wealth." His beds were adorned with gold and covered in "valuable bedding." His "clothing too was very expensive" and "much gold was expended for … [his] nourishment." Where once he had many "servants dancing attendance" on him, now he has only one. "Instead of a bath, I pour a little water on my feet and [wear] sandals on account of my weakness." The daily recitation of Psalms replaced "musicians with flute and lute" and "during the night," as he discretely puts it, he no longer commits sins but "calmly offers [his] little act of worship before taking repose." By his own account, the Roman elder is weak, and he asks his brother "not to be scandalized by my weakness."[3]

After hearing all this, the "Egyptian came to himself." This renewed self-understanding leads him not only to repentance for his own sins but also to greater appreciation for the differences in each man's situation. Reflecting on those differences the Egyptian says: "Ah me! It was from much adversity in this world that I came to be comfortable; and what I lacked then I now possess. But you came from being very comfortable into

---

3 Wortley, *Book of the Elders*, 172–73.

affliction; you came from high honor and much wealth to lowliness and poverty."[4]

I begin with this story from the desert fathers for two reasons. First, because it touches on our theme here: the relationship between asceticism[5] and our economic life. Second, the story illustrates for me the need to avoid "a common behavior of mind ... to build ... schemes far away from the annoying complexities of a familiar reality." Instead of looking at life as it is, we often seek refuge "in the future or a mythic past." In either case, we flee the here and now in pursuit of a fantasy (*prelest*) "where things have no shapes of their own" except for the one that we construct. It is this "rational scheme" that we use "as a rational model against which the disorderly architecture of today can be

---

4 Wortley, *Book of the Elders*, 173.

5 See Olivier Clément, *The Roots of Christian Mysticism: Texts from the Patristic Era with Commentary*, trans. Theodore Berkele, O.C.S.O., and Jeremy Hummerstone (Hyde Park, NY: New City Press, 1993), 130. Clément writes:

> Ascesis [the root of the word asceticism] means exercise, combat.... As free human beings with a capacity to "create positively," we are challenged to keep faith with the great transformation in Christ, such that we transform likewise, in the Holy Spirit, the relationship that in this world we necessarily have with material things—our genetic inheritance, psychological and social background—so that finally we transform the materials themselves.... Ascesis then is an awakening from the sleep-walking of daily life. It enables the Word to clear the silt away in the depth of the soul, freeing the springs of living waters ... restor[ing] to its original brightness the tarnished image of God in us.... It is the Word who acts, but we have to co-operate with him, not so much by exertion of will power as by loving attentiveness.

measured and thereby condemned."[6] When I do this, like the Egyptian monk, I risk subtly, and maybe not so subtly, standing in judgment over others for how they fail to meet my expectations about how life should be lived. Consumerism embodies just this sort of self-constructed vision.

The Loss of Authentic Ideals

Looking forward to the upcoming Great and Holy Synod of the Orthodox Church in 2016, his Holiness Patriarch Kyrill of Moscow "believes the agenda of the upcoming Council … should contain issues such as the driving of Christians from the Middle East and Northern African regions … the destruction of morals and family, and the issues of cloning and surrogate mothers." While all these matters are important, our concern here is with what his Holiness calls the "cult of consumption" that he sees as the "primary cause of the economic crisis" being experienced in many parts of the global economy.[7]

---

[6] Bertrand de Jouvenel, *The Ethics of Redistribution* (Indianapolis: Liberty Fund, 1990), 38. The term *prelest* is the Russian word for spiritual delusion. The nineteenth-century Russian Orthodox saint, Ignatius Brianchaninov, writes:

> Spiritual deception is the state of all men without exception, and it has been made possible by the fall of our original parents. All of us are subject to spiritual deception. Awareness of this fact is the greatest protection against it. Likewise, the greatest spiritual deception of all is to consider oneself free from it.

See St. Ignatius Brainchaninov, "On Spiritual Deception," *Orthodox Life*, July-August 1980, http://orthodoxleader.paradosis.com/articles/on-spiritual-deception.

[7] "Patriarch Kirill calls to speed up preparations for All-Orthodox Council," Interfax, March 11, 2014, http://www.interfax-religion.com/?act-news&div-11129.

In framing consumerism as a cult, the Patriarch has given us our starting point. Consumerism is a form of idolatry, of false worship that is the antithesis of love's voluntary self-emptying. Consumerism embodies, in the economic dimension of life, *prelest*, or as one Roman Catholic author has described it, consumerism is "the muddled idea that only in having more can we be more. Rather than the Cartesian formulation, 'cogito ergo sum' ('I think therefore I am'), some have come to believe that shopping is proof of existence '*consumo ergo sum.*'"[8]

In their 2000 document, *The Basis of the Social Concept of the Russian Orthodox Church* (hereafter, *Basis*),[9] the bishops of the Moscow Patriarchate diagnose the underlying spiritual pathology that leads us to see shopping rather than the love of God and neighbor as the confirmation of our existence and self-worth. Reflecting on the widespread problem of substance abuse among the Russian people, the synod fathers observe that the "principal reason for the desire of many of our contemporaries to escape into a realm of alcoholic or narcotic illusions is spiritual emptiness, loss of the meaning of life and blurred moral guiding lines." They go on to say that this "spiritual disease … has affected not only the individual, but also society as a whole." What is this spiritual disease? It is "the ideology of consumerism ... the cult of material prosperity." Consumerism and materialism together reflect "the lack of spirituality and the loss of authentic ideals" about what it means to be fully and distinctively human. While not "denying the need of medical aid to be given at the critical stages of drug-addiction" in the mindset (*phromena*) of the Church, "prevention and rehabilitation"

---

8 Robert Sirico, *Defending the Free Market: The Moral Case for a Free Economy* (Washington, DC: Regnery Publishing, 2012), 3–4.

9 Department of External Church Relations, *The Basis of the Social Concept of the Russian Orthodox Church* (2000), available online at https://mospat.ru/en/documents/social-concepts/.

of substance abuse and its underlying spiritual causes is "the most effective when those suffering participate consciously in the eucharistic and communal life" (11.6).

Love Is the Standard

When we think about our economic life, we might conclude that fidelity to the ascetical tradition of the Church means that we ought to consume less. It is hard, for example, to read *The Ladder of Divine Ascent* by St. John Climacus (525–606) and conclude otherwise. The saint tells us that poverty, "is the resignation of cares, life without anxiety, an unencumbered traveller, alienation from sorrow, fidelity to the commandments" (Step 17, 1) and that avarice, "or love of money, is the worship of idols [cf., Eph. 5:5], a daughter of unbelief, an excuse for infirmities, a foreboder of old age, a harbinger of drought, a herald of hunger" (Step 16, 2).[10] The negative aspect of asceticism ought not to be denied or minimized. After all, Jesus tells us to pick up our cross and follow him (Matt. 16:24; Mark 8:34; Luke 9:23). The life of Christian discipleship includes radical self-denial (Matt. 16: 25; Luke 9:24; Mark 8:35), which is to say, love. "I once saw three monks receive the same injury at the same time," writes Climacus.

> One felt the sting of this, but kept silent; the second rejoiced at his injury for the reward it would bring him, but was sorry for the wrongdoer; and the third, thinking

---

[10] St. John Climacus, *The Ladder of Divine Ascent*, trans. Archimandrite Lazarus Moore (New York: Harper & Brothers, 1959), 67, 66. Unless noted otherwise, all citations from St. John will be from Moore's translation of *The Ladder*. Page numbers will henceforth be omitted as chapter and section numbers are sufficient locative information and remain consistent across translations where included.

> of the harm his erring neighbour was suffering, wept fervently. And fear, reward and love were to be seen at work.[11]

Both in our spiritual life and in our economic life, there is "no other test in the end, nor any better expression, than our ability to love." This love must "be unselfish ... founded on respect, a service, a disinterested affection that does not ask to be paid back, a 'sympathy,' indeed an 'empathy' that takes us out of ourselves to 'feel with' the other person and indeed to 'feel in' him or her."[12] At its foundation, love is the ability to see, to affirm and to foster the uniqueness of the other person, or, as the Orthodox theologian Olivier Clément writes, love "gives us the ability to discover in the other person an inward nature as mysterious and deep as our own, but differently willed to be so by God."[13]

To be sure, love is a standard I more frequently honor in theory than in practice not only in my economic life but in my dealings with people in other areas. Yet, for all my failures love remains the standard. The primacy of love is also why I think the ascetical tradition of the Orthodox Church has an important role to play in helping us understand the moral parameters of our economic life.

The Ascetical Life

His All-Holiness Ecumenical Patriarch Bartholomew warns us that "when we fall into the trap of accepting a worldview based exclusively on *homo oeconomicus*—in other words, when human nature is understood in purely materialistic terms—it can

---

[11] Climacus, *The Ladder*, 8.27.

[12] Clément, *The Roots of Christian Mysticism*, 270.

[13] Clément, *The Roots of Christian Mysticism*, 270.

prove extremely difficult to resist the uncontrollable impulse of unrestrained acquisitiveness, which is one of the most pervasive and powerful phenomena in our secular age."[14] He goes on to acknowledge that while "[r]eligious leaders and believers may not be able to take drastic steps to correct this trend," they may be able to "sensitize and move consciences" and in so doing help individuals and communities "take measured practical steps with potentially unlimited consequences." He goes on to identify these unlimited consequences with "a change in our way of perceiving the world."[15]

Such a change is precisely what the ascetical life offers us. While we often associate asceticism with abstention (with giving things up), in the tradition of the Orthodox Church asceticism functions more as a hermeneutic of desire.[16] Through a life of private and liturgical prayer, fasting, almsgiving, and manual labor we become increasingly free from the passions or what the Orthodox theologian Dimitru Staniloae calls those thoughts, desires, and actions that "tear [us] to pieces."[17] To live under the sway of the passions means that we "live according to the senses" gradually "chang[ing] the whole [person] into 'body.'" The passionate individual is the one who lives solely "by the senses penetrated by desire and anger" to such a degree that he

---

[14] Patriarch Bartholomew, *Encountering the Mystery: Understanding Orthodox Christianity Today* (New York: Doubleday, 2008), 165–66.

[15] Bartholomew, *Encountering the Mystery*, 166.

[16] Robert M. Doran, "The Nonviolent Cross: Lonergan and Girard on Redemption," *Theological Studies* 71 (2010): 46–61. See also, John R. Friday, "Religious Experience, the Hermeneutics of Desire, and Interreligious Dialogue," *Theological Studies* 74 (2013): 581–604.

[17] Dumitru Staniloae, *Orthodox Spirituality: A Practical Guide for the Faithful and a Definitive Manual for the Scholar*, trans. Archimadrite Jerome (Newville) and Otilia Kloos (Wilkes Barre, PA: St. Tikhon Seminary Press, 2003), 93.

"is always ahead of himself," living not by hope but in a "fear (*Angst*) ... [that feeds on his] belonging to the world."[18] The hallmark of a life gripped by the passions is a crippling uncertainty in the face of the myriad possibilities which life offers. This anxiety is "nourished by the feeling that he is at the mercy of his responsibilities. [That he has] to forever launch out toward [some] future possibilities, in other words, towards [some] more appropriate opportunity."[19]

Materialism is the contemporary justification for the passionate life and whether we call it materialism or consumerism or the passionate life, freeing ourselves from its crippling grip requires a kind of knowledge that is not merely theoretical but practical. Asceticism is the practical knowledge that teaches me to act on my desires in a manner that fosters not only my own flourishing and growth in holiness but that of my neighbor as well. Seen in this way, according to Patriarch Bartholomew, asceticism is not simply a matter of our personal piety but one of the "most politically significant step[s]" we may take. As we overcome, by God's grace and our own efforts, the effects of sin in our lives, we are reformed and transformed from "mere spectators"[20] standing passively on the border into joyful men and women of faith who are willing and able, as he says elsewhere, to "free[ly] cooperat[e] with God's divine will in all areas of life including the economic dimension."[21]

The difference between materialism and asceticism highlights for us that consumerism—seeking our identity in shopping—is symptomatic of "a restless spirit that is never content with any particular material thing." William T. Cavanaugh is correct when he says that in "this sense, consumerism has some affinities with

---

18 Staniloae, *Orthodoxy Spirituality*, 106.

19 Staniloae, *Orthodoxy Spirituality*, 116.

20 Bartholomew, *Encountering the Mystery*, 166.

21 Bartholomew, *Encountering the Mystery*, 68.

Christian asceticism, which counsels a certain detachment from material things." Consumerism is my willing enslavement to my own, ever-shifting wants and desires as my will "continually moves ... from one product to another"[22] or, to use more classically Orthodox language, from one thought (*logismos*) to another. In any case, as my own inner freedom diminishes, I become less and less able to give myself away in love.

Asceticism, on the other hand, fosters in us the ability to sacrifice ourselves in love for the sake of others. Again, this is very different from seeing asceticism simply as giving things up or getting by with less. Yes, material simplicity is often part of ascetical struggle, but *foundationally* asceticism is about learning to sacrifice one's self in love. The "effective, transformative change in our world," says Patriarch Bartholomew, will only happen "when we are prepared to make sacrifices that are radical, painful, and genuinely unselfish." He concludes by observing, "If we sacrifice little or nothing, we shall achieve little or nothing."[23]

---

[22] William T. Cavanaugh, *Being Consumed: Economics and Christian Desire* (Grand Rapids: Eerdmans, 2008), xi. Compare Jesus' words in the gospel of Matthew,

> When an unclean spirit goes out of a man, he goes through dry places, seeking rest, and finds none. Then he says, "I will return to my house from which I came." And when he comes, he finds it empty, swept, and put in order. Then he goes and takes with him seven other spirits more wicked than himself, and they enter and dwell there; and the last state of that man is worse than the first. So shall it also be with this wicked generation. (Matt. 12:43–45)

[23] Bartholomew, *Encountering the Mystery*, 67. The ascetical teaching of the Orthodox Church finds an interesting parallel in recent research on the relationship between giving and human happiness. See for example, Arthur C. Brooks, *Gross National Happiness: Why*

For the tradition of the Orthodox Church, asceticism is simply living out the gospel in the context of the ebb and flow of daily life.[24]

> Then Jesus said to His disciples, "If anyone desires to come after Me, let him deny himself, and take up his cross, and follow Me. For whoever desires to save his life will lose it, but whoever loses his life for My sake will find it. For what profit is it to a man if he gains the whole world, and loses his own soul? Or what will a man give in exchange for his soul? (Matt. 16:24–26)

Left unchecked by ascetical struggle, the decisions of our economic life obscure for us what we all already know deep down: It is only when "we sacrifice our life and our belongings" that we are able to "gain life in abundance and enrich the entire world." Such, according to His All-Holiness, is the deeper experience of sacrifice: "voluntary self-emptying brings self-fulfillment."[25]

Taking Up Our Cross

The Lutheran pastor, theologian, and martyr Dietrich Bonhoeffer, writing in *The Cost of Discipleship* makes much the same point as His All-Holiness. "If there is no element of asceticism in our lives, if we give free rein to the desires of the flesh (taking care of course to keep within the limits of what seems

---

Happiness Matters for America—and How We Can Get More of It (Philadelphia: Basic Books, 2008).

[24] For more on this, see Georges Florovosky, "The Ascetic Ideal and the New Testament," in *The Collected Works of Georges Florovsky*, vol. 10: *The Byzantine Ascetic and Spiritual Fathers* (Vaduz, Germany: Buchervertriebsanstalt, 1987), 17–59. http://www.romanity.org/htm/flo.01.en.the_ascetic_ideal_and_the_new_testament.01.htm.

[25] Bartholomew, *Encountering the Mystery*, 68.

permissible to the world), we shall find it hard to train for the service of Christ." Bonhoeffer's observation is one that could be embraced by any of the Church fathers: "When the flesh is satisfied it is hard to pray with cheerfulness or to devote oneself to a life of service which calls for much self-renunciation."[26]

Even though we are damaged by sin, we are still created in the image of God and are called to live in a personal likeness of the Holy Trinity. This means that human consumption is still oriented toward communion even if my personal decisions about how to use the world often lead me astray. Asceticism is the acknowledgement that while sin often causes me to miss the mark I am able to still reorient myself toward communion with God.

Seeing the damage sin has done to our economic life and the economic systems that we have built, some Christians have advocated for a "third way" between the free market and socialism.[27] While we may praise the intention, the idea of a third way in economics is intellectually confused and unworkable in practice. What advocates of some third-way systems overlook is that there is a difference between the rule of law—of the state's prohibiting theft and enforcing contracts—and the assertion that property is owned by the state and thus has the right to exercise control over all property. The right to private property is an affirmation that there are limits to the authority of the state relative to the rights of citizens. However attractive such

---

[26] Dietrich Bonhoeffer, *The Cost of Discipleship*, trans. R. H. Fuller (New York: Simon & Schuster, 2012), 169.

[27] I am thinking here specifically of distributism, which "is often presented as a Christian 'third way' between capitalism and socialism." See Evangelical Philosophical Society, "Is Distributism a Viable 'Third Way'?: Interview between Kishore Jayabalan and Joseph E. Gorra," http://www.epsociety.org/userfiles/Interview%20with%20Kishore%20Jayabalan.pdf.

an economic system might seem, in the final analysis any such system that asserts that there is no such thing as private property (because in principle at least, all property is commonly owned by the state) is simply not compatible with the moral tradition of the Church.

There is, however, a third way that is a part of that moral tradition, the ascetical life. Christian asceticism is not a "synthesis of right-wing economic and left-wing social policies."[28] Rather, it is a third way because it is the way of the cross. Why the cross? Because, as St. Athanasius says, "It is only on a cross that a man dies with his hands spread out." Jesus spreads out his hands on the cross so that "with the one he might draw the ancient people, and with the other those from the Gentiles, and unite both in himself."[29] The cross is the true *via media*, the true Golden Mean that Aristotle says we must walk between the extremes of life.

The centrality of the cross is illustrated in the hymns for the third Sunday of Great Lent (Sunday of the Veneration of the Holy Cross). Take, for example the words we hear at Vespers:

> Come, Adam and Eve, our first Mother and Father! You fell from divine glory through the envy of Man's murder. The pleasure of the Tree of old was bitter, but see, the honored Tree of the Cross draws near! Run with haste and embrace it in joy, crying out with faith: "You are our help, most precious Cross! We eat your fruit and gain

---

28 Norberto Bobbio and Allan Cameron, *Left and Right: The Significance of a Political Distinction* (Chicago: University of Chicago Press, 1997), 8.

29 St. Athanasius, "On the Incarnation," in *Christology of the Later Fathers*, trans. Archibald Robertson, ed. Edward Rochie Hardy (Philadelphia: Westminster Press, 1954), 79.

> incorruption! We are restored again to Eden, having received great mercy![30]

The next morning at Matins we discover that from the cross shines "the brightness of Christ's Resurrection" and that we are to "draw near and kiss it with great rejoicing in our souls!"[31]

The cross represents not only Christ's sacrifice but mine as well. Just as in Adam "I died through a tree," in Christ I "have found a tree of life." Through his cross, Christ is revealed as "my invincible protector and strong defense against the demons." The "Precious Cross," so we pray, is "the Pillar of the Church, the confirmation of the faithful, the pride and salvation of those who fast."[32] Asceticism is nothing more or less than taking up the cross of Christ in my own life.

Where We Are Heading

To help flesh out the relationship between consumerism and asceticism, the next chapter will examine one of the most important ascetical saints in the Christian Church—East and West—St. Mary of Egypt. Although known for her rigorous asceticism, Mary's example illustrates for us the original purpose of human consummation as a means of communion with God, neighbor, and creation. Because she lived in a way that might be a bit distant from the life that most of us live, I then complement our examination of Mary with a consideration of

---

[30] Vespers, Sunday of the Veneration of the Holy Cross, http://www.fordham.edu/Halsall/basis/triodion/lent3sat.txt.

[31] Canticle One, Matins for Sunday of the Veneration of the Holy Cross, http://www.fordham.edu/Halsall/basis/triodion/lent3sun.txt.

[32] The Praises, Matins for Sunday of the Veneration of the Holy Cross, http://www.fordham.edu/Halsall/basis/triodion/lent3sun.txt.

the ascetical character of marriage and family life. What we will see here is that, properly understood, asceticism is able to create wealth and that this is not only morally good but it is also part of the divine plan.

Living as we do in a fallen world, this original, divinely given purpose is often frustrated in practice. Thus, chapter 2 will look at Orthodox criticisms of the free market. While often correct as far as they go, Orthodox critics of the free market often make unwarranted assumptions about the market economy. Left uncorrected, this may cause us to overlook the universal character of consumerism and, in so doing, confuse desire with greed and consumption with destruction.

A faulty understanding of the market will lead us to offer solutions to consumerism that are simply ineffective. As chapter 3 will demonstrate, while consumerism is a problem, curtailing consumption as such is not the solution because consumerism is only accidently related to abundance or scarcity. To see this requires that we properly understand the relationship between consumption and production. While in consumerism we produce in order to consume, this is to invert the order. We do not produce to consume; we consume to produce.

It is not laws and regulations that we need to reform but the human heart. Therefore, chapter 4 turns to the ascetical reformation and transformation of the human heart. Of specific interest is the Orthodox understanding that ascetical practice both builds on and finds its fulfillment in the sacraments. While all the sacraments have implications for ascetical struggle, it is baptism and especially the Eucharist that figure most prominently in our ascetical restoration of desire.

Having seen that, as with all sin, consumerism is about the misuse of our freedom, chapter 5 briefly explores the implications of asceticism for our economic life. What I hope will become clear is that, at its core, consumerism is a form of idolatrous self-worship. This is important because, as the conclusion will show, we are often tempted to substitute one form of idolatry for another. Specifically, I have in mind those who seek to impose by regulation an ideological solution to consumerism rather than foster and promote the ascetical virtues essential to a rightly ordered economic life.

I want to make sure this last point is clear.

I am not opposed to regulation. As an Orthodox Christian, I think civil law plays an important role in human society. I would even go so far as to say that Church and state—each within their own spheres and in mutual respect and deference for one another's rights and responsibilities—should work in partnership with each other. While state authority is necessary in a fallen world, it is limited, and it is limited both because our world is fallen *and* because this world (and so the state) is passing away.[33] In the theology of the Church, the state exists "not to turn the world lying in evil into the Kingdom of God, but to prevent it from turning into hell" (*Basis* IV.2). Asceticism, and so an ascetical response to consumerism, is an appeal to the human heart. As Metropolitan Kallistos puts it, we are appealing to the "mystery, freedom, relationship, and wholeness" that together constitute the human person.[34] Tempting though

---

[33] William Cavanaugh argues in *Migrations of the Holy: God, State, and the Political Meaning of the Church* (Grand Rapids: Eerdmans, 2011) that the temporal, and so temporary, nature of the City of Man is key to Saint Augustine's understanding of how the Church must relate to the state. He writes that for Augustine "the city of God makes use of the same temporal goods as does the earthly city, but in different ways and for different ends." This means that there can be "no division between earthly goods and heavenly goods, secular and sacred; there is no sphere of activities that is the peculiar responsibility of the earthly city" and not also the Church (57).

[34] Metropolitan Kallistos Ware, foreword to *Encountering the Mystery*, by Bartholomew, xix.

it is to do otherwise, we ought not to sacrifice human freedom in the service of a supposed moral good.

Chapter 6 will examine more concretely, if all too briefly, the implications for our economic life of the ascetical disciplines (prayer, fasting, almsgiving, and manual labor) and the monastic vows (poverty, chastity, obedience, and stability).

Finally, in the conclusion, I sketch out in broad terms an understanding of the free market that is compatible with the tradition of the Orthodox Church. Often, critics of consumerism assume—wrongly as I will demonstrate later—that it is somehow unique to a market economy. While there are a number of reasons for this, chief among them are the arguments unwisely used by apologists for the free market. My own experience in talking about economic ethics with Christian clergy and lay theologians has led me to see that another reason is a sloppy understanding of what we do—and more importantly *do not*—mean when we talk about the market as "free."

II Christian Spirituality and Our Economic Life

Introduction

While we will spend a fair amount of time on the subject, our primary concern in this chapter is not with marriage and family life. Rather, beginning with the life of St. Mary of Egypt, we will see how our "original hunger" has become something other than an experience of communion with God. Living in a fallen world, this original, divinely given purpose is often frustrated in practice; consumption has become a cruel parody of communion. At the same time, and again thanks to the example of our mother among the saints, Mary of Egypt, we will see that Christian asceticism can serve not only as the means of restoring this communion but also as a source of the wealth we need to be faithful to our human and Christian vocations in order to foster human flourishing and to grow in holiness.

The Orthodox theologian Fr. Alexander Schmemann's reflections on Great Lent will understand, in a practical and everyday fashion, the negative side of consumption. His work will also point us to the family as the ascetical community that fosters what the economist Jennifer Roback Morse identifies as the virtues necessary for human flourishing and a just society. Chief among these virtues is love. This last point will become especially clear when we look at the Orthodox understanding of marriage and family life embodied in the wedding service.

Desire Purified

Mary's Life

Known for, among other things, her life of severe ascetical self-denial, the example of the sixth-century monastic saint, Mary of Egypt (d. 522), might at first seem to recommend to us a model of asceticism that emphasizes abstinence—of having and using less. As we sing in one of the hymns for her feast day,

> The image of God was truly preserved in you, O mother, For you took up the Cross and followed Christ. By so doing, you taught us to disregard the flesh, for it passes away; But to care instead for the soul, since it is immortal. Therefore your spirit, O holy Mother Mary, rejoices with the Angels.[1]

As the hymn suggests, the association of Mary with strict fasting and voluntary poverty is certainly a reasonable conclusion and one I think we ought not to dismiss out of hand. Simplicity of life is foundational both to human flourishing and Christian holiness. Yet if we pay careful attention to the events of her life chronicled for us by her biographer St. Sophronius (d. 638), Patriarch of Jerusalem, a more nuanced lesson comes into focus. The saint's life illustrates not only the importance of self-denial but also how ascetical struggle can transform our consumption to an act of communion.

Mary of Egypt is a beloved saint in the Orthodox Church. Her memory is celebrated not only on April 1 but also on the fifth Sunday of Lent, on which day, in remembrance of an event toward the end of her life, it is customary for the priest to bless dried fruit after the Divine Liturgy. Every year on Thursday of the fifth week of the Great Fast (Lent), Orthodox Christians

---

1 Troparion for the Venerable Mary of Egypt, http://oca.org/saints/troparia/2014/04/01/100963-venerable-mary-of-egypt.

(and Byzantine Catholics) will gather in church to listen to a reading of Mary's life. From her biography, we know that she was a repentant prostitute who after her baptism lived a life of strict asceticism in the desert for almost fifty years. It is not an exaggeration to say that Mary was as extreme in her asceticism as she was in her sin.

In her *Vita* we discover that Mary's life of prostitution was not motivated by economic necessity; what she did, she did not for monetary gain but because she took pleasure in wickedness. For Mary the degradation of others—even at cost to her own dignity—was the goal. In her own words to the monk Zosimas, she said:

> My native land, holy father, was Egypt. Already during the lifetime of my parents, when I was twelve years old, I renounced their love and went to Alexandria. I am ashamed to recall how there I at first ruined my maidenhood and then unrestrainedly and insatiably gave myself up to sensuality. It is more becoming to speak of this briefly, so that you may just know my passion and my lechery, for about seventeen years, forgive me, I lived like that. I was like a fire of public debauch. And it was not for the sake of gain—here I speak the pure truth. Often when they wished to pay me, I refused the money. I acted in this way so as to make as many men as possible to try to obtain me, doing free of charge what gave me pleasure. Do not think that I was rich and that was the reason why I did not take money. I lived by begging, often by spinning flax, but I had an insatiable desire and an irrepressible passion for lying in filth. This was life to me. Every kind of abuse of nature I regarded as life.[2]

---

2 St. Sophronius of Jerusalem, "The Life of Our Holy Mother Mary of Egypt," in *The Great Canon: The Work of Saint Andrew of Crete* (Jordanville, NY: Holy Trinity Monastery, 2005), http://www.fordham.edu/halsall/basis/maryegypt.asp. All quotes from Mary's *Life* are from here.

Having listened to her life in church and read it several times on my own, I have come to see St. Mary not simply as a sinful woman but as someone who is deeply troubled and who because of her own suffering is willing to exploit the weakness of others. Her sin is a sin against chastity not just in terms of her sexual promiscuity but in the more foundational sense as well. If, according to Adrian von Kaam, a "chaste, or respectful, love is a love purified" of all that is self-aggrandizing "and disrespectful of concerns of others,"[3] at this point in her life Mary embodies an attitude that reflects wanton disrespect for her own dignity and that of those she misused: an unchaste, impure love—if a love at all.

Chastity is that virtue that refuses to exploit for one's own advantage the weakness of others. In this sense, chastity is not unrelated to the wholesome sense of competition we hope to see in sports or business. Healthy competition does not exploit others; rather the other person's strength or success is an invitation for me to excel—to develop more fully the talents and gifts God has given me. Therefore, Mary is not competitive in this way but unchaste; she exploits the weaknesses of others and fails to accept her life, and theirs, as gifts to be "accept[ed] and affirm[ed] … wholeheartedly."[4]

Hearing of a pilgrimage to Jerusalem to venerate the true cross, Mary decides to go along. She does not go, however, out of piety but to degrade the other pilgrims. Mary's willingness to exploit others is so deeply rooted, so much a part of her character that she is willing even to twist the things of God and turn the noble sentiments of others against them. "[O]ne summer," she says,

---

3 Adrian van Kaam, *Formation of the Human Heart* (New York: Crossroad Publishing, 1986), 47.

4 van Kaam, *Formation of the Human Heart*, 48.

> I saw a large crowd of Lybians and Egyptians running towards the sea. I asked one of them, "Where are these men hurrying to?" He replied, "They are all going to Jerusalem for the Exaltation of the Precious and Lifegiving Cross, which takes place in a few days." I said to him, "Will they take me with them if I wish to go?" "No one will hinder you if you have money to pay for the journey and for food." And I said to him, "To tell you truth, I have no money, neither have I food. But I shall go with them and shall go aboard. And they shall feed me, whether they want to or not. I have a body—they shall take it instead of pay for the journey." I was suddenly filled with a desire to go, Abba, to have more lovers who could satisfy my passion.

At this point, we might wonder: What has Mary of Egypt to do with consumerism?

Mary and Consumerism

In Mary we see both the consequence of unrestrained desire (passion) and of the possibilities for human flourishing inherent in ascetical self-mastery. While I do not think the free market, the creation of wealth, and the pursuit of profit are necessarily sinful—far from it in fact—I do know that like the rest of human life our economic life is disfigured by sin. Like Mary, all of us must take up the cross, learn "to disregard the flesh, for it passes away," and "care instead for the soul since it is immortal," as her hymn above puts it. While different in the severity of the disciplines I adopt, like Mary I must learn to discipline my appetites and desires and so purify the myriad plans and projects that make up my everyday life.

What makes Mary's life especially interesting for our discussion of consumerism is not so much the specific details of her asceticism but their results. We see these in a small, easily overlooked detail toward the end of her life. Speaking about the beginning of her life in the desert, Mary tells Zosima, through whom her story is told,

> After finishing the loaves I had, of which I spoke, for seventeen years I have fed on herbs and all that can be found in the desert. The clothes I had when I crossed the Jordan became torn and worn out. I suffered greatly from the cold and greatly from the extreme heat. At times the sun burned me up and at other times I shivered from the frost, and frequently falling to the ground I lay without breath and without motion.

She goes on to recount how she "struggled with many afflictions and with terrible temptations." In spite of all this, however, she remains steadfast in her trust and confidence in God, who she says from the very beginning of her desert sojourn "in numerous ways had guarded my sinful soul and my humble body." Therefore, she concludes,

> When I only reflect on the evils from which Our Lord has delivered me I have imperishable food for hope of salvation. I am fed and clothed by the all-powerful Word of God, the Lord of all. For it is not by bread alone that man lives. And those who have stripped off the rags of sin have no refuge, hiding themselves in the clefts of the rocks. ([cf.] Job 24; Heb. 11:38)

Let us pause here for just a moment.

Like the critic of free markets who sees the pursuit of wealth as necessarily immoral, we would be wrong if we concluded from Mary's life that desire for the good things of the creation is somehow also sinful. Yes, Mary's attitude and use of things of this life was often sinful—grossly so in fact—but look what we see on the last day of her life.

A year after their first meeting, Zosimas returns to the desert to bring Mary Holy Communion; this is only the second time in her life that she receives the Eucharist, the previous time was at her baptism almost fifty years earlier. After reciting the Creed and the Lord's Prayer, Mary receives Holy Communion and then, "rais[ing] her hands to heaven and with tears in her eyes," she repeats the Prayer of St. Symeon: "Now lettest Thou Thy servant depart in peace, O Lord, according to Thy word; for my eyes have seen Thy salvation" (cf. Luke 2:29–30). Although it is not clear at the time, when Mary asks Zosimas to bring her Holy Communion when next they meet this was her "last request." Mary knows she will die the following year, so she wants to receive the Eucharist one last time.

As part of his preparations to meet Mary, Zosimas places "some of the most pure Body and Blood into a small chalice." He then does something unasked for by the saint. He puts "some grains and dates and lentils soaked in water into a small basket," and he brings these with him. What happens next, while easy to overlook, is important: "[H]e showed her the basket, while she just touched the lentils with the tips of her fingers, and taking three grains said that the Holy Spirit guards the substance of the soul unpolluted."

Through repentance, the grace of Holy Baptism and Holy Communion, as well as her own ascetical struggle, Mary is progressively restored to a communion with Christ that is not narrow but expansive. Socially and cosmologically catholic (in the sense of holistic and universal), and in no way sectarian in her outlook, Mary illustrates the "potentially unlimited consequences" that Patriarch Bartholomew says comes when we change "our way of perceiving the world."[5] The fruit of ascetical purification and of right relationship with God is a heart that can embrace both neighbor and creation and do so in a way that depends on, rather than distracts from, the love of God.

---

5 Patriarch Bartholomew, *Encountering the Mystery: Understanding Orthodox Christianity Today* (New York: Doubleday, 2008), 166.

Called to Engage and Shape Creation

Created Hungry

This might seem counterintuitive, if not actually nonsensical, but I would suggest that Mary's life illustrates Jesus' words in the gospel that "whoever desires to save his life will lose it, but whoever loses his life for My sake will find it" (Matt. 16:25). Looking a bit more closely at Mary's example, we see that saving her life means not just restoring her relationship with God, but it also means reordering her desires and her relationship with her neighbor. What saving her life does not mean is that her desires are somehow obliterated or that she no longer has room in her life for friends. Instead, the social and material dimensions are restored to their proper places in Mary's life.

Leaving aside for now the life of St. Mary and turning to the Scriptures, this all makes good sense. Look at what happens when God establishes the human family in the garden. He turns to the man and the woman and says, "See, I have given you every herb that yields seed which is on the face of all the earth, and every tree whose fruit yields seed; to you it shall be for food" (Gen. 1:29). Whatever else might be true about us—and we will get to that in a moment—eating or, if you will, *consuming* the good things of the earth, is intrinsic to being human. Reflecting on this primordial anthropological fact, Schmemann observes that foundational to our nature and our personal identity is a certain kind of emptiness. Humanity, he writes, "is presented, first of all, as a hungry being." From the beginning,

> Man must eat in order to live; he must take the world into his body and transform it into himself, into his flesh and blood. He is indeed that which he eats, and the whole world is presented as one all-embracing banquet table for man. And this image of the banquet remains, throughout the whole Bible, the central image of life. It is the image of life at its creation and also the image of

> life at its end and fulfillment: "… that you eat and drink at my table in my kingdom."[6]

Even in our fallen condition, eating is more than merely a concession to the demands of our physical nature. In the Scriptures, food, and the entire material world is God's gift to us. Everything, Schmemann argues, "is both God's gift to man, and it all exists to make God known to man, to make man's life communion with God." Seen in light of the Incarnation, and especially the Eucharist, the whole of creation "is divine love made food, made life" for us. "God blesses everything He creates, and, in biblical language, this means that He makes all creation the sign and means of His presence and wisdom, love and revelation: 'O taste and see that the Lord is good.'"[7]

The human person "is a hungry being," and what we hunger for is God. Though Schmemann might have been startled to hear me say it, he draws from this a most Augustinian conclusion:

> All desire is finally a desire for Him. To be sure, man is not the only hungry being. All that exists lives by "eating." The whole creation depends on food. But the unique position of man in the universe is that he alone is to *bless* God for the food and life he receives from Him. He alone is to respond to God's blessing with his blessing.[8]

Our Place in Creation

The first time we see our "original hunger" is when God brings the newly created animals "to Adam to see what he would call them. And whatever Adam called each living creature,

---

6 Alexander Schmemann, *For the Life of the World: Sacraments and Orthodoxy* (1963; repr., Crestwood, NY: St Vladimir's Seminary Press, 1988), 11.

7 Schmemann, *For the Life of the World*, 14.

8 Schmemann, *For the Life of the World*, 14–15, emphasis in original.

that was its name. So Adam gave names to all cattle, to the birds of the air, and to every beast of the field. But for Adam there was not found a helper comparable to him" (Gen. 2:19–20).

St. John Chrysostom (347–407) says that the names Adam gave the animals "remain up to the present time" and that they serve as "a constant reminder of the esteem" humanity had "from the outset ... from the Lord of All."[9]

St. Ephrem the Syrian (306–373) develops a similar theme. He says that in bringing the animals to Adam, God reveals not only the creation to Adam but also Adam to himself and his place in the creation order: "Moses said, 'God brought them to Adam.' This happened in order that God might make known the wisdom of Adam and the harmony that existed between the animals and Adam before he transgressed the commandment." Not only do the animals come "[w]ithout fear" to Adam, they do so without being "afraid of each other" so that a predator "would pass by" an animal that would otherwise be its prey.[10]

In the beginning, our consumption (and the pursuit of our own self-interest that consumption embodies) did not disrupt the peace of creation. More importantly, our original hunger—and so our consumption—served the whole creation, fostered its growth, and revealed its nature.

But there is more to the story....

---

[9] St. John Chrysostom, *Homilies on Genesis, 14:20* in *Genesis 1–11*, ed. Andrew Louth, vol. 1 of *Ancient Christian Commentary on Scripture: Old Testament*, ed. Thomas C. Oden (Wheaton: IVP Academic, 2001), 65. Hereafter *ACCS: OT.*

[10] St. Ephrem the Syrian, *Commentary on Genesis*, 2.9.3 in *Genesis 1–11*, vol. 1 of *ACCS: OT*, 65.

Marriage, Family Life, and Our Communion with God and Creation

Created Lonely

God sees in the newly created man what Adam does not (at first) see in himself—that he is profoundly lonely. It is only after he engages and shapes the world around him that Adam comes to realize that for all the beauty, wonder, and goodness of creation there is not a "help meet" for him (cf. Gen. 2:20 KJV). It is through a life of prayer and creative engagement with the creation (i.e., work) that Adam comes to know himself and to know his need for human companionship. It is in response to Adam's new self-understanding that God creates the woman Eve: "And the Lord God caused a deep sleep to fall on Adam, and he slept; and He took one of his ribs, and closed up the flesh in its place. Then the rib which the Lord God had taken from man He made into a woman, and He brought her to the man" (Gen. 2:21–22).

Among other things, what makes the fall so tragic is that the relationship between Adam and Eve has been damaged. In the beginning their relationship was more than simply a practical partnership; there is nothing of mere expedience in their relationship. Rather it was a true communion (*koinonia*) and cooperation (*synergia*) between equals.[11]

---

[11] For St. John Chrysostom, this original unity between husband and wife is still obtainable within the sacrament of marriage. He refers to the union of husband and wife as a *synousia*—literally, a union of nature—a word he also uses for the relationship of persons in the Holy Trinity. For more see Vigen Gurion, "An Ethic of Marriage and Family," in *From Christ to the World: Introductory Readings in Christian Ethics*, ed. Wayne G. Boulton, Thomas D. Kennedy, and Allen Verhey (Grand Rapids: Eerdmans, 1994), 322–30.

The subservience that the animals show to Adam is absent in the relationship between Adam and Eve. Together as equals they give a humanly meaningful shape to the creation. St. Ephrem elaborates that in their shared work, "the woman was very diligent; she was also attentive to the sheep and cattle, the herds and droves that were in the field." Side by side, she would work with Adam helping him "with the buildings, pens, and with any other task she was capable of doing." The saint goes on to say: "The animals, even though they were subservient, were not able to help with these things. For this reason God made for the man a helper who could be concerned for everything for which God himself would be concerned. She would indeed help him in many things." He concludes: "He who was one in that he was Adam" had now become two, because he has "been created male and female."[12]

What are we to make of this?

Consumption and the Human Vocation

Taken in its totality, the creation of Adam and Eve suggests that human consumption is part of a larger pattern that includes not only the physical act of eating but also work, marriage, and family life. As a whole, these manifest our absolute (or ontological) dependency on God; our *relative* (or empirical) dependency on the world of persons, events, and things; our *aspiration* for a way of life that transcends the merely physical and functional dimensions; and, finally, our *enduring desire* (even if hidden for a time) for God. While there are many ways of expressing this, we can say that human beings are called to be the priests, prophets, and rulers of creation and that humanity's triple vocation is rooted in Christ and finds its fulfillment in him.[13]

---

[12] *Commentary on Genesis* 2.11, quoted in vol. 1 of *ACCS: OT*, 69.

[13] On a related note, Fr. Michael Butler and Prof. Andrew Morriss offer an exploration of this threefold human vocation and how it

If we stop here, we open ourselves to the criticism George Orwell makes of Gandhi's form of asceticism—it is merely a means of trying "to escape from the pain of living, and above all from [the hard work of] love."[14] We cannot romanticize the human condition. Doing so makes Christian theology just another ideology that seeks to obscure what we know from everyday life. Work as well as marriage and family life are often not experiences of communion. Work is often mere drudgery. As for marriage, any absence of love is keenly and painfully felt. Yet, if we are to understand the moral foundations of our economic life and what it means to experience consumption as a mode of communion, we need to turn now to the Church's understanding of marriage and what I would call the conjugal foundation of our economic life.

The Conjugal Foundation of Our Economic Life

Family and the Free Market

"In the Orthodox world view," writes Fr. Schmemann, "the home and the family constitute the first and most important area of Christian life, of *application* of Christian principles to daily existence." He goes on to say that "not the school, not even the Church" is able to form our orientation to the world of persons, events, and things as deeply and pervasively as does

---

shapes our relationship to the creation in the context of their work on environmentalism. See Michael Butler and Andrew P. Morriss, *Creation and the Heart of Man: An Orthodox Christian Perspective on Environmentalism*, Orthodox Christian Social Thought, vol. 1 (Grand Rapids: Acton Institute, 2013), 68–90.

14 George Orwell, "Reflections on Gandhi," in *George Orwell: A Collection of Essays* (Orlando: Houghton Mifflin Harcourt, 1981), 177.

"the home, the very style and spirit of family life."[15] What makes these observations especially important for our concerns here is that they are offered within the context of Schmemann's meditations on how we can apply "the Church's teaching about Lent" to our own lives so that they have "not only a nominal but a real impact … on our existence."[16]

When he wrote these words toward the end of the 1960s, many already felt the effects of urbanization and globalization, and Schmemann, while not wanting to reject the positive elements of contemporary society, was concerned that Orthodox Christians respond wisely to the challenges that these social phenomena presented. To his observation that "the whole style of family existence has been radically altered by radio and television," we can add the changes brought about by the Internet and smartphones that bring the "whole world … within my reach." As a consequence, if I am not careful, "little by little, the elementary experience of … 'interiority,' simply disappears."[17]

While not proposing any specific solutions to the spiritual challenges we face (with "no 'clear-cut recipe'"), Schmemann

---

[15] Alexander Schmemann, *Great Lent: Journey to Pascha* (Crestwood, NY: St Vladimir's Seminary Press, 1974), 100.

[16] Schmemann, *Great Lent*, 87.

[17] Schmemann, *Great Lent*, 101. In a talk given to the Zograf monastery in Greece, His Holiness Patriarch Kyrill comments on the dangers of Internet for monastics.

> Many monks act, in my view, quite unreasonably. On the one hand, [monks] leave the world in order to create favorable conditions for salvation, and on the other hand, they take their mobile telephone and start to enter the Internet where, we know, there is a large number of sinful and tempting things.

Quoted in Megan Davies, "Head of Russian Church Urges Monks to Shun Internet," *Reuters*, June 8, 2013, http://www.interaksyon.com/infotech/head-of-russian-church-urges-monks-to-shun-internet.

does return us to what we might call the first principles of Christian life reflected in Great Lent. Chief among these is the importance of carefully and critically reevaluating "the incredible superficial character of our relations with men, things, and work" that consumerism fosters. "The 'keep smiling' and 'take it easy' slogans are truly the great 'commandments'" of a life centered around shopping and the mere acquisition of wealth. What has been lost under the influence of materialistic principles "is the time for the search for *meaning*: meaning of my professional life in terms of vocation; meaning of my relationship to other persons; meaning of friendship; meaning of my responsibility."

He concludes that there "is no job, no vocation, which cannot be 'transformed'—be it only a little—in terms not of greater efficiency … but in those of human value."[18] It is this transformation that we find broadly in the ascetical tradition of the Church and concretely in the family as an ascetical community.

Writing in *Love and Economics*,[19] Jennifer Roback Morse argues that a free society, that is, a society that fosters the human flourishing of its members, depends on a particular vision of the family. It is not simply any constellation of relationships that we call "family" but the natural family that finds its source and fulfillment in procreation. It is this model of the family ("the conjugal model of marriage"[20]), where husband and wife are committed not only to each other as a married couple but to sustaining and supporting each other in their shared vocation

---

[18] Schmemann, *Great Lent*, 103–4.

[19] Jennifer Roback Morse, *Love and Economics: It Takes a Family to Raise a Village* (San Marcos, CA: Ruth Institute Books, 2008).

[20] Sherif Girgis, Ryan T. Anderson, and Robert P. George, *What Is Marriage? Man and Woman: A Defense* (New York: Encounter Books, 2012). For a concise presentation of their argument, see also Sherif Girgis, Ryan T. Anderson, and Robert P. George, "What Is Marriage?" *Harvard Journal of Law and Public Policy* 34, no. 1 (Winter 2010): 245–87.

as father and mother, that is the living source of not only a free and just society but also of those other institutions necessary to both personal and communal human flourishing. "A limited government and free market cannot exist without a substantial component of self-restraint among the citizenry." This does not just happen. The self-restraint and commitment to the common good that is needed "cannot come into existence in the absence of loving families taking personal care of their own children."[21]

What Morse is describing here is, in the Tradition of the Orthodox Church, ascetic self-denial or that self-emptying (*kenosis*) that "is the force, the 'nature,' both of the virtues, as the positive side of asceticism, as well as of the struggle against the old man, of sin." For Orthodox spirituality, says Staniloae, this process "has a Christocentric character and this Christocentricism is accentuated by the role of the mysteries [sacraments] as the means whereby Christ dwells" in us.[22]

How does the family do this? It cannot happen, Morse argues, if we "reduce family obligations to a species of contractual obligations that may be renegotiated at will by consenting adults," because the "children who result from the union are not consenting adults" and their needs "are not simply social constructs that can be redefined for the convenience of the adults." Rather, the family is based on the anthropological fact that some "childhood needs are universal and non-negotiable." Just as the free market, limited government, and "a prosperous society" requires private property rights, there are obligations that are "inherent in the relationship of parent and child." Likewise, there are virtues that "are indispensable" to the fulfillment of these obligations. Chief among these is love.[23]

---

21 Morse, *Love and Economics*, 268.

22 Staniloae, *Orthodox Spirituality*, 62.

23 Morse, *Love and Economics*, 268.

Again, for the ascetical tradition of the Church, this makes sense. Love is the goal of the ascetical life, and we demonstrate that love is at work in us precisely by our willingness to care for others. Just as marriage and family life require from us more than can be secured by contractual obligations, Staniloae reminds us that the ascetical life is not simply the "fulfillment of duties imposed by God's commands" but our "response to these commands" that bring about in us "a step by step transformation," by which we are "filled more and more with the working presence of God."[24] As we are transformed, we become more willing and able to "help our neighbors and ourselves to grow."[25] Whether in society or the family, fostering human flourishing is only possible through love, and love is only possible through ascetical self-denial. "We must prove our love for our neighbor by our work, not only in word," writes Staniloae. He goes on to say,

> The ultimate purpose of work and the taking part in the life of this world . . . is the normal development of the dormant possibilities in man and in his neighbors. Even in the enduring of troubles, which is one of the most important means of Christian striving, we don't have a running away from the life of the world, but persistence in it. The care for one's own formation and that of our neighbors, by beautifying ourselves with virtues, doesn't mean a non-participation in the life of the world. It is the very fullest collaboration, if man is part of humanity, and his formation is the ultimate goal of creation.[26]

Or as Morse writes: "Economics has been a successful social science because it focuses on things that are true: human beings

---

[24] Staniloae, *Orthodox Spirituality*, 21.

[25] Staniloae, *Orthodox Spirituality*, 44.

[26] Staniloae, *Orthodox Spirituality*, 44–45.

are self-interested and have the capacity for reason. But it is equally true that we have the capacity to love."[27]

The Orthodox Wedding Service

The ascetical formation and the practical foundation of a just society are both reflected in the Orthodox wedding service. It is in and through marriage that humanity is called by God to relate to the created order:

> God most pure, Author of all creation, through your love for mankind you transformed the rib of our forefather Adam into a woman and blessed them saying, "Increase and multiply and have dominion over the earth," and declared them both to be one through wedlock, "for because of this a man will abandon his father and mother and be attached to his own wife, and the two shall become one flesh" and "those whom God has joined together, let no human separate."[28]

The prayer then goes on to recall the exemplary married couples of the Scriptures and their role in salvation history:

> You blessed Your servant Abraham and opened Sara's womb, making him the father of many nations.
> You gave Isaac to Rebecca and blessed her offspring.
> You joined Jacob with Rachel and from him revealed the Twelve Patriarchs.
> You yoked together Joseph and Aseneth and gave them as the fruit of their union Ephraim and Manassee.

---

[27] Morse, *Love and Economics*, 268.

[28] All citations from the Orthodox wedding service are from the translation by Fr. Ephrem Lash, "Service of Crowning or Marriage," http://www.anastasis.org.uk/crowning.htm.

> You accepted Zachary and Elisabeth and declared
> their offspring to be the Forerunner.

And finally,

> You made the Ever-Virgin spring from the root
> of Jesse according to the flesh, and from her
> you became incarnate and were born for the
> salvation of the human race.

While the unitive and procreative are essential, the prayer concludes with an emphasis on the *ascetical* character of marriage and family life:

> Bless this marriage and grant to these servants of
> yours, N. and M., a peaceful life, length of
> days, chastity, love for each other in the bond
> of peace, long-lived offspring, grace in their
> children and an unfading crown of glory.
> Grant that they may see their children's children.
> Preserve their marriage bed unassailed.

The prayer then takes an interesting turn.

Amidst the concern for the soteriological and ascetical dimensions—the love between husband and wife and their vocation to be father and mother to the children God bestows—the prayer also reflects a frank, economic awareness:

> Give them of the dew of heaven from on high and
> of the richness of the earth.
> Fill their houses with wheat, wine and oil and every
> good thing, so that they may also share them
> with those in need.

In the consciousness of the Church, marriage is not only about love and babies but also the production of the wealth necessary both for the family itself *and* for the family's philanthropic vocation. For Orthodox theology the family exists not simply for itself but as the natural community through which humanity engages the created world and produces value both for its own needs and the needs of the larger human community.

This frankly economic interest is repeated in the next prayer offered by the priest on behalf of the couple. Following the same pattern as the first, the priest recalls the exemplary married couples and families not only of the Scriptures but also of Church history (e.g., Sts. Joachim and Anna or St. Constantine and his mother St. Helena who found the True Cross). Where the first prayer is limited to marriage and family life, the second prayer takes on an explicitly ascetical emphasis calling to mind as it does martyrs from both Scripture "the three holy Youths from the fire" (cf. Dan. 3:1–57, LXX) as well as Church history such as the "the holy Forty Martyrs" of Sebaste.[29] This recollection of the martyrs is important, framing the prayer's last petition that God grant the newly married couple both children and what we can only call wealth in surplus of their needs:

> Give them the fruit of the womb, fair offspring, concord of soul and body.
> Exalt them like the cedars of Lebanon, like a well-cultured vine.
> Grant them rich harvest, so that, having all sufficiency for themselves, they may overflow into every good work that is also well-pleasing to you, and that they may see their children's children like newly planted olive trees all around their table. And, having been well pleasing to you, may they shine like beacons in heaven, in you our Lord, to whom belong

[29] Commemorated March 9.

> all glory, might, honour and worship, now and forever, and to the ages of ages.

Wealth is both a blessing from God and the fruit of human labor. Important as this is, more importantly is the *goal* of wealth. The prayer asks God to make the couple biologically and economically fruitful, the latter not as an end in itself but in the service of the larger society (and especially for the poor). All of this, as the rest of the service makes clear, is the fruit of the ascetical character of marriage.[30] For our purposes here, however, what matters is that love and fidelity, marriage and family life, are not simply the lens through which the Orthodox Church understands both society and our economic life but also that this lens is ascetical.

---

30 See Paul Evdokimov, *The Sacrament of Love: The Nuptial Mystery in the Light of the Orthodox Tradition*, trans. Anthony P. Gythiel (Crestwood, NY: St Vladimir's Seminary Press, 2001), 73. This ascetical theme is also seen in the biblical reading used in the liturgy. The Epistle reading (Eph. 5:22–30) emphasizes the necessity of mutual submission of husband and wife to each other and together to Christ. The gospel reading (John 2:1–11), as the service makes clear, sees the changing of water into wine by Jesus as a symbol of the transformation of marriage as a natural institution into Christian sacrament, a relationship that reveals (and makes real) the presence of Christ in human history. Evdokimov writes,

> The wedding rite symbolically summarizes the entire married life. The betrothed have already exchanged rings; they have already been crowned and they partake of the one cup of life. It is only in the evening of life that this cup, symbolic of fullness, will be taken, when the shadow of the crowns will fall upon it … [and] the spaces of the heart that do not exist as of yet … are created by suffering. In order to be loved by the other, one must renounce oneself completely. It is a deep and unceasing ascetic practice. The crowns of the betrothed refer to martyrdom.

Conclusion

Interesting though it is, our concern here has not been with marriage and family life (at least not directly) but with exploring the spirituality that underlies our economic life. As we saw in the life of St. Mary of Egypt, our "original hunger" has become something else than an experience of communion with God. Living in a fallen world, this original, divinely given purpose is often frustrated in practice; consumption has become a cruel parody of communion. At the same time, and again thanks to the example of our Mother among the saints, Mary, we have also seen that, properly understood, asceticism can serve not only as the means of restoring this communion but also to create wealth, and that this is not only morally good but part of the divine plan.

Schmemann's reflections on Great Lent helped us see how the fallen character of our economic life plays out in an everyday fashion. He also inspires us to look to the family as the ascetical community that fosters what Morse calls the virtues necessary for human flourishing and a just society. Chief among these virtues is love. This is especially clear when we look at the Orthodox understanding of marriage and family life embodied in the wedding service.

In the next chapter, we will look at Orthodox criticisms of the free market. We need to do this not simply because we are interested in consumerism but also because the social nature of the human person, and so our economic life, is not limited to the boundaries of the family. As we will see, while correct as far as they go, Orthodox critics of the free market often make unwarranted assumptions about the market economy. Left uncorrected, this can cause us to overlook the universal character of consumerism and, in so doing, confuse desire with greed and consumption with destruction. More importantly, however, they can cause us to overlook the possibilities for human flourishing that are essential to our human and Christian vocation to love.

III Orthodox Criticism of the Free Market

Orthodox Christian Economic Vision

While I think it is one of its great strengths, Orthodox theology tends to approach even technical moral issues pastorally, casting arguments in a manner more akin to a homily than an academic argument. Frustrating though it can be, I do think this more pastoral, practical approach can vivify our discussion of consumerism and help us understand it not primarily in terms of public policy but in terms of Christian spirituality. At the same time, anyone who comes looking for a systematic treatment of economic issues, such as consumerism in Orthodox social thought (henceforth OST), will likely go away disappointed. There is value in taking a more analytical approach to consumerism. In this section we will systematize the economic observations in the *Basis* and the writing of the Ecumenical Patriarch. What we will see is that underneath these often *ad hoc* statements there is a model of economic activity rooted in the gift of God the Father offered to humanity in and through the person of Jesus Christ.

Moscow Patriarchate

Writing in the *Basis of the Social Concept of the Orthodox Church*, the bishops of the Moscow Patriarchate seek to sketch out the groundwork necessary to respond to the many social and moral issues facing the Church after the fall of communism. The concerns they address are familiar to most Western Christians: the relationship between Church and state, war and peace, marriage and family life, and bioethics and secularism. Of special concern for us here is their statements on economics, especially the human vocation to labor and the right to "the fruits of labour." Inherent in human labor is the right "to own and use property, the right to control and collect income, the right to dispose of, lease, modify or liquidate property" (*Basis*, 7.1). The bishops also affirm both technological advances and contemporary economic development. They go on to praise the "improvement of the tools and methods of labour, its division into professions" as well as overall "better material living standards."

At the same time, the bishops argue that Christians must be prudent in their embrace of these advances. In a fallen world, "people's enticement with the achievements of the civilisation moves them away from the Creator and leads to an imaginary triumph of reason seeking to arrange earthly life without God. The realisation of these aspirations in human history has always ended in tragedy" (*Basis*, 6.3). While others may disagree, I see in this a provisional affirmation by the bishops of the free market. The bishops remain cautiously mindful of what, in a 2004 statement, they call the "hard years of totalitarian atheism that subjected the faith of Christ to direct and open persecution." While thankfully "now in the past," today the "trial by violence has been replaced by the temptation" that comes with increased political and economic freedom. The bishops "note with bitterness that society seems unable to withstand" the myriad challenges of this new social situation.[1]

---

1 "Message of the Bishops' Council to the Honourable Monastics and All the Faithful of the Russian Orthodox Church," Department for External Church Relations of the Moscow Patriarchate, October 8, 2004, http://orthodoxeurope.org/page/19/2/93.aspx.

However, pastoral caution is different from condemnation of the free market. For example, in addition to the passage quoted above praising technological advances, economic developments made possible by the free market (*Basis*, 6.3), the bishops devote an entire section (*Basis*, 7) to property rights, a key part of both liberal democracy and the free market.

> Property is commonly understood as a socially recognised form of people's relation to the fruits of labour and to natural resources. The basic powers of an owner normally include the right to own and use property, the right to control and collect income, the right to dispose of, lease, modify or liquidate property. (*Basis*, 7.1)

In their treatment of both human labor and property rights, the bishops take care to remind the reader that neither human labor nor property rights are absolute. Neither can be exercised appropriately if doing so moves society "away from the Creator and leads to an imaginary triumph of reason seeking to arrange earthly life without God." When this has happened, it "has always ended in tragedy" both for individuals and the society (*Basis*, 6.3) as was so clearly demonstrated by the rise of atheistic materialism during the Soviet era.

Together with Butler and Morriss, I wish the bishops demonstrated a more sophisticated understanding of the free market and its benefits.[2] At the same time, the concern that motivates the *Basis* is pastoral not economic. In the *Basis*, the Church is responding to the challenges of a society newly freed from Communism that now faces the new challenges and temptations of secularism. In response, the Church strives to see not only the weeds but also the wheat.

---

2 Fr. Michael Butler and Andrew Morriss, *Creation and the Heart of Man: An Orthodox Christian Perspective on Environmentalism*, Orthodox Christian Social Thought, vol. 1 (Grand Rapids: Acton Institute, 2013), 7-11.

> As secularism developed, the lofty principles of inalienable human rights turned into a notion of the rights of the individual outside his relations with God. In this process, the freedom of the personality transformed into the protection of self-will (as long as it is not detrimental to individuals) and into the demand that the state should guarantee a certain material living standard for the individual and family. (*Basis*, 4.7)

Together with this benign view of human rights there has developed a parallel anthropology that situates "civil human rights" in the vision of "man ... not as the image of God, but as a self-sufficient and self-sufficing subject" (*Basis*, 4.7). It is this second, deformed and deformative vision of the human person, not the free market itself, that is the subject of the bishops' criticism.

Reflecting the Tradition of the Church, the authors of the *Basis* (4.7) reject as unacceptable an anthropology of radical self-sufficiency because apart from God, "there is only the fallen man, who is rather far from being the ideal of perfection aspired to by Christians and revealed in Christ (*'Ecce homo!'*)." In addition, because of the "Christian sense of justice, the idea of human freedom and rights is bound up with the idea of service." Therefore, any economic system or theory that fails to include the social dimension of the human person must be criticized even if it need not be wholly rejected. Unlike consumerism and its self-aggrandizing focus on the individual, his wants, and his desires, the Church teaches that the "Christian needs rights so that in exercising them he may first of all fulfil in the best possible way his lofty calling to be 'the likeness of God,' as well as his duty before God and the Church, before other people, family, state, nation and other human communities" (*Basis*, 4.7). Again, what the bishops are criticizing is not the free market as such but rather "an almost ontological individualism" that would make the individual "prior to society" and make society itself a reflection not of the communal nature of man but merely "the voluntary contract of individuals trying to maximize their own self-interest."[3]

Ecumenical Patriarch Bartholomew

His All-Holiness Ecumenical Patriarch Bartholomew offers us a nuanced understanding of economic matters in light of the Tradition of the Church. Speaking at the Plenary Assembly of the European Parliament meeting in Brussels, Patriarch Bartholomew reminded the delegates that "the concept of 'nation state' is by no means coextensive with and inclusive of the human condition."[4] This is not to suggest that the contemporary understanding of the nation is unimportant. "Nations can provide systems of economics and justice, methodologies of security and interdependence, but the sum of every part of a society never reaches the whole of the individual." Taking his lead from Plato who "sought the perfect society by looking at the condition 'writ large' of the human person," his All-Holiness goes on to say "we must discover in the human person the very qualities that will enable us to transcend division and achieve—not mere unions of cooperation, but the fundamental unity that links every person to one another."

---

3 Robert Bellah et al., *Habits of the Heart: Individualism and Commitment in American Life* (New York: Harper & Row, 1985), 143. As we have already seen, we cannot absolutely dismiss self-interest. To do so is to open the door to totalitarianism. For more on how the minimization of self-interest (leveling) can lead, sometimes with the best of intentions, to injustice, see Hunter Baker, *The System Has a Soul: Essays on Christianity, Liberty, and Political Life* (Grand Rapids: Acton Institute, 2014), 79–84.

4 "Address of Ecumenical Patriarch Bartholomew to the Plenary Assembly of the European Parliament," Brussels, September 24, 2008, http://www.archons.org/news/detail.asp?id-265.

Together with the Moscow Patriarchate, Patriarch Bartholomew would have us reject secularism, radical individualism, and materialism. While the modern, liberal, and secular state has a valuable role to play in human flourishing, in Bartholomew's view it is imperative that Christians and those of good will seek out and articulate a more transcendent, more distinctively human foundation for human society. "For dialogue to be effective" and indeed "to be transformative in bringing about core change in persons" that the Christian tradition describes as repentance (*metanoia*): "It cannot be done on the basis of 'subject' and 'object.' The value of the 'other' must be absolute—without objectification; so that each party is apprehended in the fullness of their being."

Looking more explicitly at the Church's tradition, Bartholomew suggests that it is in the "icon" that we can find that way of seeing that transcends the subject-object dichotomy as well as our tendency to see each other not as unique persons created in the image of God but in terms of rigid and objectifying categories. Many societies within the larger human community take this latter route, effectively choosing to "shun the greater whole and close themselves off from the dominant society," thus undermining any possibility of dialogue rooted "in mutual appreciation."

For this reason, Bartholomew asks us to consider the approach to dialogue embodied in the icon. For Orthodox Christians, the icon "stands not only as an acme of human aesthetic accomplishment," but it incarnates and makes present "an act of communion with the person represented in the icon." If this is true for the two-dimensional icon, "how much more should our encounters with living icons—persons made in the image and likeness of God—be acts of communion!" For this to be even possible,

> there must be a more profound understanding of the absolute interdependence—not merely of states and politi-

> cal and economic actors—but the interdependence of every single human person with every other single human person. And such a valuation must be made regardless of any commonality of race, religion, language, ethnicity, national origin, or any of the benchmarks by which we seek self-identification and self identity. And in a world of billions of persons, how is such inter-connectedness possible?

For human beings, such a tangible, global experience of "inter-connectedness" is impossible. It is only God who can experience a living communion with each and every person, "regardless of any commonality of race, religion, language, ethnicity, national origin, or any of the benchmarks by which we seek self identification and self identity."

We can nevertheless experience something of this communion in and through the "ecosphere that contains us all." While this becomes the foundation for the Ecumenical Patriarch's environmental concerns, it is not without implications for our economic life and especially for human consumption. Just as every "ecosystem on this planet is like a nation—by definition limited to a place," every ecosystem (again like every nation) "will have an effect that goes far beyond its natural—or in the case of cultures, national, boundaries." As we come to understand more fully that every ecosystem "is part of the singular ecosphere that is inhabited by every living breath that fills the world," we see as well that the whole of created being is interconnected and reflects "the powerful communion of all life, and our true interdependency on one another." For this reason,

> there must be respect for the rights of the minority within every majority. When and where the rights of the minority are observed, the society will for the most part be just and tolerant. In any culture, one segment will always be dominant—whether that dominance is based on race,

> religion or any other category. Segmentation is inevitable in our diverse world. What we seek to end is fragmentation! Societies that are built upon exclusion and repression cannot last. Or as the divine Prince of Peace said: "Every kingdom divided against itself is brought to desolation, and every city or house divided against itself will not stand" (Matt. 12:25).

Liberty, rightly understood (which is to say, sacramentally and ascetically), is essential both to human flourishing and to a just society. Unfortunately, in his address to the European Parliament, his All-Holiness offers little in the way of substantive comments about economics and its relationship to liberty, instead limiting himself to making general observations about the importance of intercultural dialogue in the European context.

However, earlier that year in an address to the Eleventh Euroasian Economic Summit meeting in Istanbul, his All-Holiness addresses the economic order more explicitly.[5] As with his remarks to the European Parliament, the environmental concerns are the context of the Patriarch's remarks about "the rightful use of the planet's energy resources, the fair distribution of material goods to overcome poverty worldwide, and the development of authentic dialogue in the pursuit of peace throughout the world." As with his address in Brussels later that year, his All-Holiness argues in Istanbul that "any appropriate response to and resolution" of "critical [environmental and economic] issues can only be anticipated when people of all disciplines and backgrounds, above and beyond racial or reli-

---

[5] "Address of Ecumenical Patriarch Bartholomew at the Eleventh Euroasian Economic Summit," Istanbul, May 3, 2008, http://www.patriarchate.org/documents/euroasian-economic-summit.

gious boundaries, meet in the earnest hope of working together for a better world." Any such discussion must be animated and guided by a courageous "hope for a world where there is enough for all people and where the world's resources are used respectfully and selflessly."

In his presentation at the Euroasian summit, Bartholomew goes on to say that all those "who believe in a living God are … called to interpret their convictions in a way that both suggests and manifests the divine wish for all people to enjoy the fruits of the earth in an equitable manner, without hurting one another and without abusing the resources of our planet." Far from existing in separate, unconnected dimensions, spirituality and economics are intimately related. Yes, the theological language of religion and spirituality may differ from "the technical vocabulary of economics and politics." But

> the barriers that at first glance appear to separate religious concerns (such as salvation and spirituality) from pragmatic interests (such as commerce and trade) are not impenetrable. Indeed, such barriers appear to crumble before the manifold challenges of social justice and globalization. Whether we are dealing with environment or peace, poverty or hunger, education or healthcare, there is today a heightened sense of common concern and common responsibility, which is felt with particular acuteness by people of faith as well as by those whose outlook is expressly secular.

The pastoral life of the Church and economic development can converge because, in the final analysis, both are concerned with—albeit under different profiles—human flourishing. Additionally, both the Church and the well-functioning market share a common anthropological foundation. This is why he reminds the Euroasian delegates that

> [i]t is at once inconceivable and incorrect that religious adherents cannot appreciate how the way we pray in churches, mosques and temples is a direct reflection of the way we live as citizens in our respective professions. And, by analogy, the way we treat other people and the natural environment on this earth is the clearest sign of just how authentically we pray to God in heaven.

We need to pause a moment and ask what this means.

Lex Orandi, Lex Credendi, Lex Vivendi

While he does not use the phrase, the Ecumenical Patriarch's argument here is an application of the patristic notion of *lex orandi, lex credendi, lex vivendi* or "how we worship reflects what we believe and determines how we will live." As the Roman Catholic deacon Keith Fournier describes it for his tradition, so also for Orthodox Christians liturgy "is not an 'add on.'" Liturgical worship is for both communities the foundation of our respective identities, "expressing our highest purpose." Worship "reveals what we truly believe and how we view ourselves in relationship to God, one another and the world into which we are sent to carry forward the redemptive mission of Jesus Christ." The Church's worship "is a prophetic witness to the truth of what she professes." How does this happen? How does "worship" serve as "a dynamic means of drawing the entire human community into the fullness of life in Jesus Christ"? Liturgy "attracts—through beauty to Beauty. Liturgical worship informs and transforms both the person and the worshipping community which participates in it." This is possible because "[t]here is reciprocity between worship and life."[6]

---

[6] Deacon Keith Fournier, "Lex Orandi, Lex Credendi, Lex Vivendi. As we Worship, So we Believe, So we Live," Catholic Online, November 8, 2010, http://www.catholic.org/news/hf/faith/story.php?id=39029. For a more extensive treatment of *lex orandi, lex*

Commenting on what he calls Dostoevsky's "enigmatic remark" from *The Idiot* that "beauty will save the world," Alexandr Solzhenitsyn in his 1970 Nobel Prize lecture, asks us to consider: "What sort of a statement is that?" Is it "mere words"—a mere sentimental statement that is impotent in the face of humanity's long and "bloodthirsty history"? Or is it possible for beauty not simply to ennoble and uplift us but actually to save us? For Solzhenitsyn, and the tradition of the Orthodox Church, the answer is a resounding, if sober, yes.

> There is, however, a certain peculiarity in the essence of beauty, a peculiarity in the status of art: namely, the convincingness of a true work of art is completely irrefutable and it forces even an opposing heart to surrender. It is possible to compose an outwardly smooth and elegant political speech, a headstrong article, a social program, or a philosophical system on the basis of both a mistake and a lie. What is hidden, what distorted, will not immediately become obvious.[7]

Solzhenitsyn provides us with the broader context within which to understand consumerism. The moral question of consumption is not "how much" we consume but to "what end" our

---

credenda, see John Meyendorff, *Byzantine Theology: Historical Trends and Doctrinal Themes* (New York: Fordham University Press, 1979), 115–25; Alexander Schmemann, *Liturgy and Tradition: Theological Reflections of Alexander Schmemann*, ed., Thomas Fisch (Crestwood, NY: St Vladimir's Seminary Press, 1990); Geoffrey Wainwright, *Doxology: The Praise of God in Worship, Doctrine, and Life—A Systematic Theology* (New York: Oxford University Press, 1980).

7 Alexandr Solzhenitsyn, "Nobel Lecture," in Nobel Lectures in Literature, 1968–1980 (River Edge, NJ: World Scientific Publishing, 1993), 34-48, available online at http://www.nobelprize.org/nobel_prizes/literature/laureates/1970/solzhenitsyn-lecture.html.

consumption serves. Is human consumption in the service of communion—the hallmark of which is beauty—or is it some other end? If the latter, then no matter how restrained, no matter how modest, no matter how financially equitable or environmentally sensitive, it is immoral.

Returning to the Ecumenical Patriarch's comments, we see precisely this point. Addressing the Euroasian economic summit he quotes "a renowned monk and mystic living in Palestine" during the sixth century, "Barsanuphius the Great." The saint says: "Not wounding my neighbor; that is the way of God!" He goes on to observe that he "can think of no better definition of religious belief and moral practice for those of us who strive to inspire our faithful in accordance to godly precepts." The desire to first do no harm is "formative for those who hold positions of leadership and responsibility, and who strive to motivate international and interdisciplinary action in response to pressing global problems." According to Bartholomew, if we build on such a foundation, then we can both respect our religious and cultural differences while at the same time "work together for the well-being of humanity and the life of the world" in a way that allows "humanity to transcend political or religious differences in order to transform the entire world for the glory of God."[8]

The Primacy of the Gift

While we need to take seriously the economic statements made by the Ecumenical Patriarch and the Moscow Patriarchate, both reiterate the theme outlined in the *Basis* that consumerism is a moral problem and a consequence of the free market.[9] At the

[8] "Address of Ecumenical Patriarch Bartholomew at the Eleventh Euroasian Economic Summit."

[9] Interestingly, the Department of External Church Relations of the Moscow Patriarchate posted a selection from a speech given

same time, the lack of technical understanding of economics can make statements such as this difficult to accept. Nevertheless, we need to bear in mind that even formal statements about morality are rhetorically more akin to an extended homily than to a work of systematic theology.[10]

For example, this applies to the 2005 Paschal message of Patriarch Alexy II of Moscow, in which he contrasts consumerism with the economy of God's gift to humanity in Jesus Christ. What is especially important for the latter is that, as his Holiness reminds us, having been "liberated from the captivity of sin" we become able to "render our life all the more beautiful, for we increase in our soul's eternal riches." The human and

---

by Pope John Paul II. In his address to the Italian Parliament on November 15, 2002, he makes an observation that will be echoed in subsequent statements and speeches from representatives of the Russian Orthodox Church:

> There is a need to guard against a vision of the Continent that would take into account only its economic and political aspects, or that would uncritically yield to lifestyles inspired by a consumerism indifferent to spiritual values.

Pope John Paul II, "Europe, Open Once Again Your Doors to Christ!" Department of External Church of the Moscow Patriarchate, December 24, 2002, http://orthodoxeurope.org/page/14/19.aspx.

[10] Given the great reliance of Orthodox theology on patristic authors, this is not surprising. In fact, some scholars have suggested that this close alliance with the early Church is a strength of Orthodox theology. See Johan Leemans and Johan Verstraeten, "The (Im)possible Dialogue between Patristics and Catholic Social Thought: Limits, Possibilities, and a Way Forward," in *Reading Patristic Texts on Social Ethics: Issues and Challenges for Twenty-First-Century Christian Social Thought*, ed. Johan Leemans, Brian J. Matz, and Johan Verstraeten (Washington, DC: Catholic University Press, 2011), 222–31.

Christian vocation to make ourselves and society beautiful is firmly rooted in the Church's experience of the Resurrection.

> The revelation that "God is love" (1 John 4:8) is the greatest gift to mankind of the Incarnate Son of God. Love transfigures, purifies and sanctifies all that is around us. And we, in following the Saviour's commandment on sacrificial, self-denying love towards people, are made a part of Divine love which, kindled in our hearts, fills our whole life with unextinguished Paschal joy. It is then that the apostle's words come true for us: "Everyone who loves is born of God and knows God" (1 John 4:7).

Having experienced the joy of the resurrection in and through the Church's liturgical worship (above all, the Eucharist), we are now able to "travel along the way of salvation diligently and unswervingly." This path however is not without its own risks.

> This way is always thorny and narrow. And it is not by chance that many around us in the world have abandoned this way, dimming their spiritual eyes by striving for power and fame, comfort and the acquisition of worldly goods, unbridled consumerism and endless trivial entertainments.[11]

The balance here is a delicate one.

When they are rooted in our faith in Jesus Christ, human and economic development are morally good and are the proper

---

[11] Patriarch Alexy II, "The Paschal Message of His Holiness Patriarch Alexy II of Moscow and All Russia to the Archpastors, Pastors, Monastics and All Faithful Children of the Russian Orthodox Church," Department for External Church Relations of the Moscow Patriarchate, May 1, 2005, http://orthodoxeurope.org/page/14/66.aspx. All quotes in this and the following paragraphs are from this source.

concern of individual Christians and the Church as a whole. Nevertheless, consumerism represents a real practical and spiritual danger for the Christian and society. "The Church knows this road [consumerism] will lead the human race down a blind alley and will never make the human race happy." For this reason fidelity to the gift given to us in Christ's resurrection requires an ascetical effort on our part. "The way of Christ" is "the way of bearing one's cross" and only subsequently "the way of resurrection." It is the cross that "lead[s] us to the light which radiates forth from the Life-Giving Tomb of the Lord." Or, to put it another way, consumerism is a way of life that undermines our ability "to vanquish all sorrow and sadness, to possess the fullness of peace and joy."

This personal, ascetical effort, if undertaken in gratitude and faith, will result not only in a personal renewal but also in a transformation in our relationships with each other. Alexy continues,

> My beloved ones! Let us, as the apostle exhorts us, "walk in a renewed life." Let us reject enmity and confrontation, sinful ways and weakness of the soul. With every day and hour of our life let us fulfill Christ's commandment: "Let your light so shine before men, that they may see your good works and glorify your Father in heaven" (Matt. 5:16).

Unlike the self-aggrandizing concerns of consumerism, the gift economy is philanthropic:

> There are in our midst many people who feel keenly the need for help and care. These are our elderly citizens, the victims of wars, crime and natural disasters, all those who suffer from disease, poverty, loneliness, homelessness and who have no parents. Let us bring to each one of them as a Paschal gift our active love, our modest contribution and labours of charity.

As with Christ, the gift economy is not limited to the visible boundaries of the Church:

> "The day of the Resurrection of our Lord Jesus Christ," writes St. John Chrysostom, "is the foundation of peace, the beginning of reconciliation, the cessation of hateful actions, the destruction of death, the defeat of the devil." May Christ's Passover bring peace where blood is shed and where hatred is kindled. May all people of the world extend towards each other the hand of brotherhood and working together for the common good. I assure everyone that the Russian Orthodox Church will labour in the name of the blessed reconciliation and the harmony of the whole human race. It is in this ministry that we remain as always open to joint labours with the state and the many and varied social forces, with peoples of different faiths and convictions.[12]

What matters for our purposes here is the contrast between consumerism as a false anthropology and asceticism as the proper lens through which to understand the person and society. We will return to this later, but, for now, we can say that unlike consumerism, asceticism fosters those habits of thought and action that in turn promote not only human flourishing and Christian holiness but also that contribute to a just and free society in which all people of good will are able to participate.

Conclusion and Transition

If we come to OST looking to find a systematic treatment of economic issues such as consumerism, we will likely be disappointed. Orthodox theology tends to approach even technical moral issues pastorally, casting arguments in a manner more

[12] Alexy II, "Paschal Message," http://orthodoxeurope.org/page/14/66.aspx.

akin to a homily than an academic argument. Frustrating though it can be, I do think this more pastoral, practical approach can vivify our discussion of consumerism and help us understand it not primarily in terms of public policy but Christian spirituality.

At the same time, I do think there is value in taking a more analytical approach to consumerism. Butler and Morriss have, I think, offered us a helpful hint here. Both the *Basis* and the Ecumenical Patriarch assume that human consumption is fundamentally destructive. Is this really true? Is consumption simply destructive? Or might it also be creative? In our next section, we will look at precisely that, the creative character of human consumption.

IV The Gift Economy and the Free Market

Before we look at the connection among greed, consumption, and consumerism, I want to spend a little time looking more closely at the economic implications of seeing creation and redemption as God's gift to us. For the Tradition of the Orthodox Church, divine grace is always only bestowed to us personally. As one of the hymns for Pentecost puts it,

> Blessed are You, O Christ our God; You have revealed the fishermen as most wise by sending down upon them the Holy Spirit[;] through them, You drew the world into Your net. O Lover of mankind, glory to You![1]

Grace, in other words, establishes a personal relationship between the Holy Trinity and the human recipient in a manner that accents rather than obscures the uniqueness of the person, his gifts, and circumstances. Alternatively, in the words of another hymn sung on Pentecost:

> The Holy Spirit is Light and Life, a living Fountain of spiritual gifts, the Spirit of wisdom and understanding, all-knowing, upright and good—He leads us and washes away our sins.

---

1 Troparion for Pentecost, http://www.anastasis.org.uk/PentAll.htm.

> He is God and he makes us divine; He is Fire proceeding from Fire, speaking and acting and distributing gifts. Through Him all the prophets, martyrs and apostles of God are crowned.
>
> Strange account, strange and wonderful sight: fire is divided for distributing gifts.[2]

While we might think of grace as abstract, airy, and insubstantial—in the consciousness of the Church, grace is anything but. Grace is manifested concretely in the life of the person, slowly transforming that life and through that life the wider communities of which he or she is a member.

We see the concreteness of grace reflected in the Church's liturgical practice. For example, in the Great Litany at the beginning of the Divine Liturgy we pray: "For travelers by land, sea, and air, for the sick, the suffering, the captives, and for their salvation, let us pray to the Lord."[3] Though bestowed on us by the God who is "ineffable" and "incomprehensible," his grace is nevertheless tangible. God has "brought us from non-existence into being, and when we had fallen away," he "raised us up again." Even in the face of humanity's persistent sin God does not "cease to do all things" for us "until [He] had brought us up to heaven, and had endowed us with [His] kingdom which is to come." After praising God at the beginning of the Anaphora in the Liturgy of St. John Chrysostom, we ever so slightly shift our focus: "For all these things we give thanks to

---

[2] Sticheron, Great Vespers for Pentecost, http://www.anastasis.org.uk/PentAll.htm.

[3] *The Divine Liturgy of St. John Chrysostom*, Greek Orthodox Archdiocese of America, http://www.goarch.org/chapel/liturgical_texts/liturgy_hchc. Variations of this petition are found several times in the Anaphora (Eucharistic Canon) of both the Liturgy of St. John Chrysostom and the Liturgy of St. Basil the Great.

You, and to Your only-begotten Son, and to Your Holy Spirit; for all things of which we know and of which we know not, whether manifest or unseen." We are called to respond with gratitude to God for all that He has given us.

The primacy of gratitude in our spiritual lives as well as the catholic scope of thanksgiving is illustrated in the athakist hymn "Glory to God for All Things."[4] Let me draw attention to one portion of the hymn. In the second half, we hear how the "breath of Thine Holy Spirit inspires artists, poets and scientists." We go on to say how God, "makes them prophets and interpreters of Thy laws, who reveal the depths of Thy creative wisdom." What's most interesting though is the hymn's assertion that "[t]heir works speak unwittingly of Thee. How great art Thou in Thy creation! How great art Thou in man!"

The wisdom and power of God is revealed "in the laws of the universe … for all nature is filled with Thy laws." Although God has "revealed to us" his mercy, he has also "hidden from us" aspects of his will as a goad to "the inventiveness of the human mind" and to make clear "the dignity of man's labour"

---

4 There are in the Orthodox Church numerous akathist services celebrated in honor of the Most Holy Trinity, the Mother of God, different saints, or events in salvation history. The Greek "akathist" means a hymn said while standing (*a-* = negation; *kathist* = sitting; thus, "not sitting") and traditionally the clergy and the faithful stand throughout the service. The akathist "Glory to God for All Things" was written by Fr. Gregory Petrov, a Russian Orthodox priest, "shortly before his death in a [Soviet] prison camp in 1940. The title is from the words of St. John Chrysostom as he was dying in exile. It is a song of praise from amidst the most terrible sufferings." For the complete text of the service see "The Akathist of Thanksgiving," The Preachers Institute, http://preachersinstitute.com/2010/11/25/the-akathist-of-thanksgiving/, from which all citations of the akathist as well as this background information are taken.

(Ikos 7). The created as much as the uncreated, the temporal and the eternal, human work and creativity as much as the divine archetype on which they are based and in which they participate—all of these singularly and together have revealed the mercy of God.

My response will always fall short of the gifts given me. Nevertheless, in the words of the akathist, I can and should ask the "Life-giving and merciful Trinity" to "receive my thanksgiving for all Thy goodness." It is in this way, through thanksgiving, that we are by God's grace "worthy of Thy blessings, so that, when we have brought to fruit the talents Thou hast entrusted to us, we may enter into the joy of our Lord, forever exulting in the shout of victory: Alleluia!" (Kontakion 13).

This akathist, like the liturgical tradition as a whole, reminds us that our gratitude must transcend our own limited awareness of what God has done for us; we receive blessings "known and unknown" as we hear in the Liturgy of St. John Chrysostom. This is why, theologically, even a "gift" between human beings "always goes *beyond* the approximate equality of values that characterizes exchange in a competitive market."[5] This transcendent quality of all gift reflects its personal character; gifts express the love between the giver and the recipient. This is important for our understanding of consumption.

Labor and the Gift Economy

Grace creates but it also transforms. We saw above that fishermen become wise, or as we hear in Vespers on Pentecost Sunday evening:

---

[5] John D. Mueller, "Finn's 'Nine Libertarian Heresies' and Mueller's First Lemma: Economists Complain Exactly Insofar as They Are Unable to Explain," *Journal of Markets & Morality* 14, no. 2 (Fall 2011): 529. Emphasis in original.

> Now the Apostles of Christ are clothed with power from on high. The Comforter is renewed in them and renews them with newness of knowledge. They preach in foreign tongues, proclaiming mystical knowledge in lofty words. They teach us to worship the Benefactor and God of all in His simple, eternal, tri-personal nature. Enlightened by their teaching, let us bow down to worship Father, Son, and Spirit, earnestly praying for salvation for our souls.[6]

Grace is creative and transformative. This is why, in the economic realm, we can (and really must) talk about wealth creation as the proper end of human labor and creativity. Let me explain.

Having spent several happy years now working with economists, I have come to appreciate how much they love thought experiments. Economist John D. Mueller challenges us to imagine a world without property rights, that is to say a world in which "God intended all … the earth's goods" to

> *be common goods*, in which everyone shared ownership indiscriminately—a sort of global communism extending Karl Marx's economic theory to the world. In such a system, neither gifts nor exchanges would exist, because no one would have any *right* to dispose of anything by either kind of transaction. To presume this state of affairs is simply factually false.[7]

Why? Because it flies in the face of the personal character of a gift. Without personal property, one would have nothing to give. So now you might be wondering, what has this to do with our economic life?

---

6 Sticheron, Kneeling Vespers for Pentecost Eve, http://www.anastasis.org.uk/PentAll.htm.

7 Mueller, "Finn's 'Nine Libertarian Heresies,'" 529.

We saw in the last chapter, that the moral tradition of the Orthodox Church affirms a fundamental *human* right to property. This reflects a more fundamental right of each person to the fruit of his or her own labor ("profit" in the broadest sense); just as God orders the primordial chaos he created out of nothing at the beginning of creation, human beings—created as we are in His image and likeness—are called to order creation according to our own creative abilities. This means that the right to property is grounded not in culture—much less in positive law—but in creation itself, or, if you prefer, in human nature itself.

> Labour is an organic element of human life. The book of Genesis says that in the beginning "there was not a man to till the ground" (Gen. 2:5). Having created the Garden of Eden, God put man in it "to dress it and to keep it" (Gen. 2:15). Labour is the creative fulfilment of man who was called to be the co-creator and co-worker of the Lord by virtue of his original likeness of God. (*Basis*, 6.1; ASV)

The pursuit of profit and the right to own property are not solely manifestations of the worker's right to the fruits of his labor. In addition, profit and property give tangible expression to the human person's vocation to be both "co-creator and co-worker" with God. Because we live in a fallen world, our pursuit of profit and our acquisition of property have both been damaged by sin. A Christian perspective on the free market and economic liberty cannot overlook or minimize the damage done by sin.[8]

---

[8] The need to take seriously the consequences of human sinfulness is a central motivation for this work. In the chapters following this, I will look more closely at both the effects of sin on human consumption ("the passions") and how we can overcome these consequences through the ascetical life.

When people unjustly pursue profits through fraudulent business practices, or when they use their property for immoral purposes, for example, they do so because human labor is not as it ought to be. "The creative component of labour," to quote Pope John Paul II, has been "weakened." He goes on to explain that this means that labor has "become mostly a means of sustenance." Living in a fallen world, the spiritual dimension of labor—how it reflects our vocation to be co-creators and co-laborers with God—is often obscured. We find ourselves working for no other reason than to keep body and soul together. When this happens, labor has become toil (i.e., work that is often boring and even humiliating). Nevertheless, though it is often obscured, the connection between consumption and communion remains because, even in a fallen world, work remains "a sharing in the activity of God the Creator."[9]

The objective goodness of human labor does not mean that, subjectively, the work we do is always morally good or at the service of human flourishing. Labor, and so our use of the fruits of our creativity and ingenuity (consumption), according to the *Basis*, are not "pleasing to God" when they serve "the egoistic interests of [the] individual or human communities ... to meet the sinful needs of the spirit and flesh." As with the rest of human life, our consumption is "blessed" only "when it represents co-working with the Lord and contribution to the realisation of His design for the world and man." The twofold goal of our labor ("co-laboring" with God and human flourishing within the context of the natural law) sets the *minimum* standard for how we use the fruits that flow from it. Concretely this means that we are called by God to work "to sustain [ourselves and our

9 Pope John Paul II, encyclical letter *Laborem Exercens* (September 14, 1981), 25, http://www.vatican.va/holy_father/john_paul_ii/encyclicals/documents/hf_jp-ii_enc_14091981_laborem-exercens_en.html.

family] without being a burden for others." We are also called to create wealth over and above what we need so that we can "give to the needy" (*Basis*, 4.4). As we said in our reflections on the conjugal basis of our economic life, *self-sufficiency* and *philanthropy* together represent the goal of human labor and consumption.

Profit, Property, and the Gift Economy

For the tradition of the Church, the problem is not that we consume, that we pursue profit, or that we own property. No, the moral problem is that human labor and the use of its fruits are unmoored from our original communion with God. The gift of creation and redemption at the heart of Orthodox cosmology and anthropology does not do away with our need to work. Much less does it do away with a right to private property or the moral goodness of creating wealth. Profit and property are good and serve our nonnegotiable moral obligations to be productive. Put somewhat differently, the ability to create wealth (profit) and to acquire and develop property are all given to us by God so that we can support ourselves and our families. Following from this, they are also given to us so that we are able "to take care of those who for various reasons cannot earn their living, such as the weak, the sick, strangers (refugees), orphans and widows." This second point is why the Church "in defence of the voiceless and powerless … calls upon society to ensure the equitable distribution of the fruits of labour, in which the rich support the poor, the healthy the sick, the able-bodied the elderly" (*Basis*, 4.6).

In both cases, the wise use of material blessings requires that we cultivate a spirit of gratitude or thanksgiving for the gifts we have received.[10] For example, as part of the celebration of

---

[10] This is why we find a variety of blessings in the *Book of Needs* (from the Slavonic *Trebnik* or in Greek, *Euchologion*, literally "book of prayers").

Theophany (in the West the Baptism of Our Lord), the priest will bless water asking that God the Father "[s]end down the grace of the All-holy Spirit upon this water, and bless, purify and sanctify it with Your heavenly benediction, and grant unto it the grace and blessing of Jordan, and the power of purification of all impurity, and expelling of demons and all their assaults and snares."[11]

As part of the domestic celebration of the feast, the priest will also bless the homes of his parishioners. Following the pattern that we saw in the marriage ceremony, the importance of the private home in salvation history is recalled:

> "O God our Savior, the True Light, Who were baptized in the Jordan by John to renew all people by the waters of regeneration, and Who condescended to enter under the roof of Zacchaeus, bringing salvation to him and to all his house." The prayer goes on to ask that "[a]s the same Lord, also keep safe from harm those who dwell here; grant to them Your blessing, purification and health of body; grant all their petitions that are for their salvation and eternal life."[12]

There are other blessings—for the meat and dairy products that break the long Lenten fast on Pascha (Easter); for grapes on the Feast of the Transfiguration; for flowers on the Dormition (Assumption) of the Mother of God; for the first fruits of the harvest; and for salt, farm animals, apiaries, and automobiles. Over all of these, the Church invokes the blessing of God and expresses the gratitude of the human heart for gifts received. In all these and like blessings, the prayers of the Church show us

---

11 "The Sanctification of Water in Brief" in *A Priest's Prayer Book*, ed. David F. Abramtsov and Daniel Swires (1971; repr., Thompson Ridge, NY: St. German's Chapel Press, 2006), http://www.stluke-orthodox.com/html/liturgicaltexts/priestsprayerbook.cfm.

12 "A Form for Blessing Homes at Theophany" in *A Priest's Prayer Book*.

the object being blessed within the context of salvation history. Far from being at odds with spiritual concerns, the material world, human labor, wealth, and property are all revealed to be intimately and necessarily connected to humanity's redemption and "the mystery of His will, according to His good pleasure which He purposed in Himself, that in the dispensation of the fullness of the times He might gather together in one all things in Christ, both which are in heaven and which are on earth—in Him" (Eph. 1:9–10).

We must be careful, however. The Church is speaking here *theologically* and *pastorally*. We cannot directly draw concrete policy recommendations from the Church's life. OST affirms that the "spiritual welfare and survival of society are possible only if the effort to ensure life, health, and minimal welfare for all citizens becomes an indisputable priority in distributing the material resources." This obligation flows from—but does not negate—property rights. Rather, "[t]he Church urges Christians to see in property"—and by extension all wealth both material and social—"God's gift given to be used for their own and their neighbours' benefit" (*Basis*, 7.2). Especially in light of the abuses against the human right to property and the resulting "social upheavals and people's suffering," Orthodox Christians

> cannot approve the alienation and re-distribution of property with violations of the rights of its legitimate owners. An exception may be made only for the alienation of property based on the law, conditioned by the interest of the majority of people and accompanied by fair compensation. Russian history has shown that the violation of these principles has always resulted in social upheavals and people's suffering. (*Basis*, 7.3)

While the Church affirms the moral legitimacy of profit and property, this is firmly rooted in the social character of the human person and does not imply the kind of radical, ontological individualism that we saw above.

The question, however, remains: How am I to meet my obligation "to sustain" myself and my family "without being a burden for others" while at the same time caring for the poor (*Basis*, 6.4)? How, in other words, do we balance self-interest and altruism?

Self-interest, Altruism, and Greed

Especially in the popular imagination, we are used to speaking about self-interest in terms of greed, and certainly greed is something that we need to guard against. However, we need to also guard against reducing self-interest to greed. I will say more about this in a moment; for now, though, I want to draw your attention to an interesting observation in the *Basis* about fulfilling our obligations to care for those who cannot care for themselves. These are found at the end of the section titled "Church and Politics" (5.4).

While not all are morally obligated to do so, some among the laity are called to participate directly "in the work of legislative, executive and judicial bodies and political organisations." Historically Orthodox Christians have done so "under various political systems, such as autocracy, constitutional monarchy and various forms of the republican system." Even when "non-Christian rule and the regime of state atheism" make "participation of the Orthodox laity in civic and political processes ... difficult," the laity are still called to serve *as best as they are able* according to "the gospel's morality" to promote and balance the demands of "truth and mercy (Ps. 85:10)." Those among the laity who do work in politics or in the public square are to be guided by a "concern for the spiritual and material welfare of people, the love of the fatherland and the desire to transform the surrounding world according to the word of Christ."[13] This is a bold statement on the part of a Church that has suffered horribly under Communism. Yes, there are immoral laws and even immoral governments, but this does not mean that Christians should withdraw from political life. Rather, in faith, hope, and love, we are to bring the world around us into conformity with the gospel.

At the same time, the Church is aware that government service—even when directed toward objectively moral and praiseworthy goals—is not without its own risks. Chief among these is the temptation to forsake the common good (even if unwittingly) and instead adopt policies that "tend to benefit only a part of society, while restricting or infringing upon the interests and wishes of others. Many such decisions and actions are stained with sin or connivance with sin. Precisely for this reason the Orthodox politician or statesman is required to be very sensitive spiritually and morally."[14] What does this have to do with our concern with helping others? Just this:

> The Christian who works in the sphere of public and political building is called to seek the gift of special self-sacrifice and special self-denial. He needs to be utterly attentive to his own spiritual condition, so that his public or political work may not turn from service into an end in itself that nourishes pride, greed and other vices.

---

[13] Compare this to Jeremiah 29:5–7:

> Build houses and dwell in them; plant gardens and eat their fruit. Take wives and beget sons and daughters; and take wives for your sons and give your daughters to husbands, so that they may bear sons and daughters—that you may be increased there, and not diminished. And seek the peace of the city where I have caused you to be carried away captive, and pray to the Lord for it; for in its peace you will have peace.

[14] Crony capitalism is an example of the moral vice the Church is warning against here.

Greed is not simply a temptation in the economic sphere; greed for social capital (especially at public expense) is also something we must guard against. The bishops go on to quote St. John Chrysostom's admonishment to rulers. "A true king," the saint says, "is he who conquers anger and jealousy and voluptuousness and subjects everything to the laws of God and does not allow the passion for pleasure to prevail in his soul." Chrysostom concludes that it is just such a person he would like to see "in command of the people, and the throne, and the cities and the provinces, and the troops." Why this person? Because "he who subjected the physical passions to reason would easily govern people also according to the divine laws." As for the greedy ruler, "he who appears to command people but in fact accommodates himself to wrath and ambition and pleasure ... will not know how to dispose of the power."

The Morality of the Free Market

Hearing all this, we might think that while the free market has done a good job in generating wealth it has done so by fostering immorality or at least not correcting immorality.[15] As should be clear by this point, I do not think the free market is a panacea; it is not as if all our personal and social problems will be solved if we embraced a *laissez faire* approach to the marketplace. Nevertheless, I am frankly skeptical of those who argue that socialism (whatever they mean by this) is a morally better way of organizing our economic life.

Let me explain.

Writing in *Why Not Capitalism?* Jason F. Brennan observes that we often "insert evil motivations into the very definition"

---

[15] See, for example, Luigino Bruni and Robert Sugden, "Reclaiming Virtue Ethics for Economics," *Journal of Economic Perspectives* 27, no. 4 (Fall 2013): 141–64, available at http://pubs.aeaweb.org/doi/pdfplus/10.1257/jep.27.4.141.

of the free market. He asks us to imagine Adam Smith saying, "By 'socialism,' I just mean a system of bloodthirsty dictators who starve and slaughter peasants." Hearing this we would know immediately that the speaker was being unfair and that his argument is "both bad philosophy and bad lexicography."[16] Yet even advocates of the free market will assume that "[c]apitalism works better only because it harnesses our greed and fear." As for socialism this, or at least its advocates assume, "is the system of love and community." While moral failures in the marketplace are seen as somehow inherent to a market economy, this is not so with socialism. Why? Because (as the thinking goes) "[s]ocialism is not bad for us—we are bad for socialism."[17] Critics and defenders alike seem to be united in their assumption that the free market "works better than socialism ... only because we are not kind and generous enough to make socialism work. If we were saints, we would be socialists."[18]

This moralizing way of describing the free market and socialism is not helpful. It obscures the fact that "[c]apitalism and socialism are simply ways of organizing the ownership of property. In capitalism, individuals may own the means of production. In socialism, they may not—the means of production are owned collectively (or by the representative of the collective, such as the State)." To advocate, as I am here, for the free market as the context for human consumption is to advocate for a social system that "has private property in the means of production," where "decisions about the use of property are made by owners rather than by governments or society at large," where "people may make contracts as they please," and where (ideally, at least)

---

[16] Jason F. Brennan, *Why Not Capitalism?* (New York: Routledge: Taylor & Francis Group, 2014), 64.

[17] Brennan, *Why Not Capitalism?*, 7

[18] Brennan, *Why Not Capitalism?*, n.p.

"legal monopolies and subsidies are absent."[19] More importantly for our interest here, as we have seen already, OST views as morally good what Brennan describes as constitutive of a free-market economy.

Contrary to what I sometimes hear, affirming the moral legitimacy of the free market is not the same as defending moral relativism in the economic order. The market does not "merely normalize egoism" but also fosters "genuine virtues that can be upheld with authenticity."[20] As we saw above, for OST the constitutive elements of the free market—the pursuit of profit, wealth creation, and private property—are all in and of themselves morally good. Yes, as the Church points out, there are times when people pursue profit or acquire property in ways that are contrary to the gospel, but this is a failure of the person and not of the market itself. One of the reasons I think this distinction can be difficult to grasp is because we forget that, as Brennan puts it, "[s]ocialism is not equality or community. It's just a way of distributing the control rights over objects." We need to be very careful of the tendency to ignore the presence of human sinfulness and assume that socialism is all about "love ..., kindness ..., generosity," and "oceans of delicious lem-

---

19 Brennan, *Why Not Capitalism?*, 63–64.

20 Bruni and Sugden, "Reclaiming Virtue Ethics for Economics," 160. The market virtues they identify are universality, enterprise, and alertness; respect for the tastes of one's trading partners; trust and trustworthiness; acceptance of competition; self-help; nonrivalry; and stoicism about reward (154–60). According to Jönsson, "Review of The Bourgeois Virtues," McCloskey identifies the virtues of hope (optimism, entrepreneurship), faith (identity, integrity, loyalty, honesty), love (benevolence, friendship, *agape*), justice (social balance and honesty), courage (autonomy, daring, endurance), temperance (individual balance and restraint, humility), and prudence (know-how, foresight, *phronesis*) as all intrinsic to a morally sound and economically productive free market.

onade." Although the last of these is not representative and is particularly silly, it was the prediction of the "utopian socialist Charles Fourier," who firmly believed "that under socialism we would transform the oceans into lemonade."[21]

This is not to say that there are not moral failures in the free market; there are. However, to argue that "the market economy makes people greedy, selfish, and amoral is," according to Herbert Gintis, "simply fallacious." Far from simply creating an environment of moral coarseness, "religious and lifestyle tolerance, gender equality, and democracy have flourished and triumphed in societies governed by market exchange, and nowhere else."[22] Seen in light of the Church's tradition, not all of these developments are of the same moral weight or equally welcome—ours is after all still a fallen world, and, even in the most justly ordered free society, we cannot escape the consequences of human sinfulness. On balance, however, the assertion that the free market is itself a source of moral failure is simply false.

Looking at the social changes brought about by a market economy, Luigino Bruni and Robert Sugden caution that we need to keep in mind "that virtues are defined relative to practices. The traits that make a person good *as a participant in markets* need not be evaluated positively in all domains of human life." This means that while there is such a thing as a virtuous market economy, the market is not "the only morally relevant domain" or that "the market virtues are the only virtues." At the same time, we ought not to think "that the market virtues apply only within the practice of the market." Market virtues can also "apply in other domains of human life that are understood

---

[21] Brennan, *Why Not Capitalism?*, 64. As Brennan summarizes the matter, Fourier "was a bit of a nut." His comments about Fourier and lemonade are found in note 19.

[22] Herbert Gintis, "Giving Economists Their Due," *Boston Review*, June 25, 2012, quoted in Brennan, *Why Not Capitalism?*, 66.

as cooperation among equals for mutual benefit." The market is only "one part of the network of cooperative relations of which civil society is made up.... This means that the market virtues are also virtues of civil society in general" and that virtues from other domains of human life (e.g., family or religion) are also (or at least can be) market virtues. Thus, tolerance, to take one example, in the market place will likely take a different form in the Church or civil society.[23]

As with virtue, so also with vice. While we often see individuals in the free market pursuing profit at the expense of their neighbor or the common good, Brennan reminds us that "socialist economies are not free of predation, greed, and fear. Quite the contrary."[24] The darker motives "of greed and fear" are as prominent in socialist economic systems as in a free market economy. The difference is that, in a socialist context, they are less likely to be motivated by individualism and more likely to take a collectivist form. This means that we will see "greed on behalf of, and fear for the safety of, one's family" rather than on behalf of the individual. More treacherously, a collectivist appeal to greed or fear or any other vice might seem to defend a traditional or communal way of life when in fact this is not the case. As Brennan writes,

> Even when one has wider concerns than one's mere self, the socialist position is greedy and fearful in that one's fellow socialist citizens are predominantly seen at best as possible sources of enrichment and at worst as threats or mouths to feed. These are horrible ways of seeing other people, however much we have become habituated and inured to them after a century of socialist civilization.[25]

---

[23] Bruni and Sugden, "Reclaiming Virtue Ethics for Economics," 160–61.

[24] Brennan, *Why Not Capitalism?*, 64.

[25] Brennan, *Why Not Capitalism?*, 35–36.

Our concern here, however, is not socialism but the challenge of consumerism in a free market. What our examination of socialism has demonstrated is that sentimentality and romanticism are not commensurate with sound moral reasoning about our economic life. As with a host of other social ills in other contexts, consumerism reminds us that all is not well with how we exercise our economic and social freedoms in the context of a market economy. Regardless of the system within which we pursue our economic life, we will be tempted by sin. For the moral philosopher or theologian, the real challenge is avoiding making sin—rather than virtue—the analytical touchstone of his work.

In the next chapter, I want to examine greed and envy a bit more closely. Specifically I want to offer an alternative to the negative view of human consumption that critics as well as apologists of the free market too often assume. While the history of this particular—and erroneous—line of thinking is beyond what we can do here, I do think it is worth looking at two seminal figures in the history of economic thought: the mid-twentieth-century economist and retail analyst Victor Lebow and the late nineteenth- and early twentieth-century economist and sociologist Thorstein Veblen. These two thinkers illustrate the analytical dangers inherent in looking at our economic life through the lens of a warped anthropology that sees consumption as foundationally destructive rather than productive. Specifically, I will argue that we see greed as essential to the free market because we make a prior—erroneous—assumption that human consumption is not in the service of communion but is of a disunity rooted in either the self-aggrandizing tendencies of the individual or the collectivist tendencies of the group.

V Consumption: Vicious and Virtuous

Reshaping a Distorted Anthropology

During Matins for the Feast of the Annunciation, there is a delightful exchange between the Virgin Mary and the Archangel Gabriel that illustrates for us the importance of discernment in the spiritual life. While the Annunciation's focus is significantly different from the economic matters that concern us here, the discussion between Mary and Gabriel can be of use for us nonetheless.

The liturgical conversation begins immediately after the Angel's greeting and proclamation that Mary is to bear the Christ Child. The Virgin responds,

> O Angel, help me to understand the meaning of thy words! How shall what thou sayest come to pass? Tell me clearly, how shall I conceive, who am a virgin maid? And how shall I become the Mother of my Maker?

Gabriel's response leaves no room for doubt as to what Mary is saying:

> Thou dost think, so it seems, that I utter words deceitfully; and I rejoice to see thy prudence. But take courage,

> O Lady: for when God wills, strange wonders are easily accomplished! (Ode 1)[1]

Yes, God can work wonders; Mary does not doubt this. Her concern is different:

> When she accepted the suggestion of the serpent, my mother Eve was banished from divine delight. Therefore I fear your strange greeting, for I take care that I not slip. (Ode 3)

It is only after closely questioning Gabriel that the Virgin is satisfied that his words are true, and she expresses her willing submission to God's will.

> Receiving your glad tidings, O Gabriel, I am filled with divine joy for you speak to me of a joy that has no end! (Ode 6)

Being joyfully obedient to God's will for her life does not mean that the Virgin has surrendered her caution. Even though obedient, Mary is concerned (as she says to Gabriel) lest she be deceived "as Eve was deceived." The reason for her hesitancy—even in the midst of joy—is understandable enough. As she says to the Angel:

> Childbirth comes from mutual love: such is the law that God has given to men.... I know not at all the pleasures of marriage: how then doest thou say that I shall bear child? I fear lest thou speakest guile. Yet lo, thou criest out: O all ye works of the Lord, bless ye the Lord! (Ode 8)[2]

---

[1] Mother Mary and Kallistos Ware, trans., *The Festal Menaion* (South Canaan, PA: St. Tikhon's Seminary Press, 1990), 449.

[2] Mother Mary and Ware, *Festal Menaion*, 456.

Again, mindful of the significant difference between the events recorded in Luke 1:26–38 and our interest here in economics, the conversation illustrates for us the importance of discernment in the spiritual life even when, and maybe especially when, we are doing good.

To help us reshape a distorted anthropology and come to a critical—but appreciative—understanding of human consumption, we need to look with a discerning eye at our economic life. As we saw in the last chapter, even proponents of a market economy tend to argue that it functions primarily because of greed. While we certainly do see the morally deforming effects of greed, this is only part of the story. The generally accepted view of both critics and apologists that a market economy functions by tolerating vice obscures the moral foundation of the free market. Given the arguments made by its advocates, I think critics can be forgiven when they argue that the free market does not foster virtue and merely exploits our sinful tendencies to greed and self-aggrandizement.

While the history of this particular—and erroneous—line of thinking is beyond what we can address here, I do think it is worth looking at two seminal figures in the history of economics whose work lends itself to thinking of the market as rooted in vice: the mid-twentieth-century economist and retail analyst Victor Lebow and the late nineteenth- and early twentieth-century economist and sociologist Thorstein Veblen. These two thinkers' works can help us understand the danger of looking at the market and our economic life primarily in terms of the consumption of wealth rather than its creation.

For OST, the essential elements of the free market (profit, private property, and economic development) are morally good, but they must be rightly used. While the fathers of the Church are suspicious of the wealthy,[3] their concern is not with the moral goodness of wealth as such but that it not be pursued for its own sake (greed) or used for the self-aggrandizement (pride and vain glory) of its owner. Instead, wealth is to be used for the good of humanity (especially the poor). To borrow from one of the desert fathers, Abba Moses, greed, pride, and vainglory are the "spurious" motivations for the pursuit of wealth. We need to be careful, however, that in rejecting sinful motivations and goals, we do not embrace an antidevelopment mentality. Both are "fake and counterfeit coinage," but while the former is clearly wrong, the latter represents a more traitorous temptation for Christians—having the "appearance of piety" while lacking the substance of real wisdom.[4]

Economic development that violates the gospel—or what I think is in its own way worse, failing even to uphold basic human rights and decency (natural law)—is the "viciously heretical stamp on the precious gold" (referring again to Abba Moses) not simply of Scripture but of our economic life. At the same time, trying to correct immoral modes of economic development by rejecting *all* development is to make use of "underweight coins"

---

[3] See, for example, Helen Rhee, "Wealth, Poverty, and Eschatology: The Pre-Constantine Christian Social Thought and the Hope of the World to Come," in *Reading Patristic Texts on Social Ethics: Issues and Challenges for Twenty-First-Century Christian Social Thought*, ed. Brian Matz, Johan Leemans, and Johan Vertraeten (Washington, DC: Catholic University Press, 2011), 79.

[4] Quoted in John Cassian, *Conferences*, trans., Colm Luibheid (New York: Paulist Press, 1985), 57. Cassian's conferences are a series of dialogues featuring famous hermits of the Egyptian desert. It is not always entirely clear (as with Plato and Socrates, for example) whether what one reads is meant to really be the words of the hermit in question or is Cassian speaking through a particular historical character. As Cassian attributes the words to Abba Moses (the Ethiopian), however, I do so here as well.

that are "dangerous and inadequate" to the needs of the poor and the fundamental goodness of wealth and property.[5] Whether we are talking about immoral development or an ideological rejection of morally good development, we are held captive by "thoughts which have lost weight and value because of the rust of vanity, thoughts which do not measure up to the standard of the ancients"[6] who had a catholic vision of the human person and thus the morally good use of wealth. To help us clear away the rust, let us turn now to Lebow and Veblen and see what they can help us discover about our economic life.

Vicious Consumption

Lebow: Production Is for Consumption

Victor Lebow, in his article "Price Competition in 1955,"[7] argues that the free market is motivated by greed. While his argument has some merit, it can easily mislead us as we work to understand the ethical challenges facing our economic life in the context of a free market. Specifically, I have in mind his assumption that consumption is the key to the free market's success. If we make *consumption*, rather than *virtue*, the engine that drives our economic life, then I think the Church is right to be skeptical of the free market itself. However, what if the

---

5 Henry DeSoto, in *The Mystery of Capital: Why Capitalism Triumphs in the West and Fails Everywhere Else* (New York: Basic Books, 2000), argues that legal barriers that prevent people from securing (and so exercising) property rights to which they have an informal claim is a key reason why many of the world's poor are unable to rise out of poverty.

6 Cassian, *Conferences*, 57.

7 Victor Lebow, "Price Competition in 1955," *Journal of Retail*, 31, no. 1 (Spring 1955): 5–10, http://hundredgoals.files.wordpress.com/2009/05/journal-of-retailing.pdf.

market not only fosters virtue but also requires it? What if, as economist Deirdre McCloskey has argued, "without virtue the machinery of neither the market nor the government works for our good"?[8]

Lebow's work certainly encourages skepticism that the free market is an arena for developing virtue. For example, his contention that mid-twentieth-century American capitalism's "enormously productive economy demands that we make *consumption our way of life*, that we convert *the buying and use of goods into rituals*, that we seek our *spiritual satisfactions*, our *ego satisfactions*, in consumption." As we will see, though Lebow is wrong in asserting that consumption *alone* drives the free market he is partially correct when he says,

> The measure of social status, of social acceptance, of prestige, is … to be found in our consumptive patterns. The very meaning and significance of our lives today [is] expressed in consumptive terms. The greater the pressures upon the individual to conform to safe and accepted social standards, the more … he tend[s] to express his aspirations and his individuality in terms of what he wears, drives, eats, his home, his car, his pattern of food serving, his hobbies.[9]

For Lebow, it is axiomatic that a growing capitalist economy needs "things consumed, burned up, worn out, replaced, and discarded at an ever increasing pace." For this reason "commodities and services must be offered to the consumer with a special urgency." He goes on to say that the market economy as it existed in the 1950s requires "not only 'forced draft' consumption, but 'expensive' consumption as well." Hence, while

---

[8] Deirdre McCloskey, *The Bourgeois Virtues: Ethics for an Age of Commerce* (Chicago: University of Chicago Press, 2006), 49.

[9] Lebow, "Price Competition in 1955," 7.

the free market helps us meet our basic physical and social needs[10]—to "eat, drink, dress, ride, live"—it requires us to do so "with ever more complicated and, therefore, constantly more expensive consumption. The home power tools and the whole 'do-it-yourself' movement," concludes Lebow, "are excellent examples of 'expensive' consumption."[11] We will come back to this point later, but for now we can say that Lebow is correct that the free market has a *moral* foundation even if he is wrong in his assertion that consumption is its central moral imperative.

Veblen: "Conspicuous Consumption"

To be fair to the critics, greed is a problem in the free market. Think about department store customers rioting on Black Friday as they push, shove, and trample each other in order to buy a deeply discounted flat screen television. While we are at it, what does it say about the store and the corporation that owns it that—knowing what has happened in years past—they continue to hold these kinds of sales? Yes, I know that people are responsible for their actions; and yes, I know that in a fallen world greed is a constant. However, the fact that human beings are sinful and that business can make a profit from sin is not a compelling defense for a market economy. Granted, no one is (necessarily) arguing that this kind of unrestrained greed is a good thing. The fact that my neighbor sins does not excuse my sin; much less does it justify my making a profit by exploiting his moral weakness.

---

[10] On this, compare the hierarchy of needs in Abraham Maslow, "A Theory of Human Motivation," *Psychological Review* 50, no. 4 (1943): 370–96, http://psychclassics.yorku.ca/Maslow/motivation.htm, as well as idem, *Motivation and Personality* (New York: Harper & Row, 1954).

[11] Lebow, "Price Competition," 7–8.

While there are significant differences between what we see on Black Friday and the consumption that Lebow says drives a market economy, both are modes of *conspicuous consumption*, a term that the economist and sociologist Thorstein Veblen (1857–1929) introduces in his book, *The Theory of the Leisure Class: An Economic Study of Institutions*.[12] While a complete criticism is beyond our scope here, given the significance of his work in the popular understanding of economics, I think a few observations are in order. [13]

Let us begin by asking: Why do we want things?[14] Veblen argues that we want things because in "order to gain and to hold the esteem of men it is not sufficient merely to possess wealth or power. The wealth or power must be put in *evidence*, for esteem is awarded only on evidence."[15] In other words, I want things to show off and to show up my neighbor; my consumption is motivated by pride, vainglory, and a desire to inspire envy in others. My consumption is inherently self-aggrandizing.

Veblen is correct when he says that decisions about consumption are meant to signal the status of the person and that they help to sketch out the boundaries of a community. We desire and use goods to create, communicate, and confirm our personal identity and place in the community. This is why we can say

---

[12] Thorstein Veblen, *The Theory of the Leisure Class: An Economic Study of Institutions* (New York: Penguin Books, 1994), available online at http://www.gutenberg.org/ebooks/833.

[13] See Hunter Baker. "Reflections on Social Justice, Government, and Society," *Journal of Markets and Morality* 15, no. 1 (2012): 143–59, http://www.marketsandmorality.com/index.php/mandm/article/view/689.

[14] This is the question that Mary Douglas and Baron Isherwood explore in *The World of Goods: Towards an Anthropology of Consumption* (New York: Routledge, 1979).

[15] Veblen, *The Theory of the Leisure Class*, 36, emphasis added.

with him that all decisions about leisure or consumption are "conspicuous." Veblen is also correct in saying that, like manners and decorum, economic decisions "are an expression of the relation of status—a symbolic pantomime of mastery on the one hand and of subservience on the other."[16] His argument becomes more problematic and less useful for understanding consumerism when he says that conspicuous leisure and consumption, manners and decorum, serve to insulate the wealthier members of society from the poorer neighbor and to enforce this distinction to the harm of the latter and the advantage of the former.

Leaving aside his assertion that the "possession of wealth … was at the outset valued simply as an evidence of efficiency," it is certainly true that being wealthy is

> in popular apprehension, itself a meritorious act. Wealth is now itself intrinsically honourable and confers honour on its possessor. By a further refinement, wealth acquired passively by transmission from ancestors or other antecedents presently becomes even more honorific than wealth acquired by the possessor's own effort.[17]

What he describes, however, is not limited to a particular social class or to "a later stage in the evolution of the pecuniary culture,"[18] which he equates with industrialization in general and capitalism in particular. Critically, Veblen reduces the social function of consumption simply to self-aggrandizement. He overlooks the fact that discrete segments of a society are constituted not simply by the consumption decisions of other segments but also by their own internal decisions about the relative value of particular goods and ways of spending time.

---

[16] Veblen, *The Theory of the Leisure Class*, 47.

[17] Veblen, *The Theory of the Leisure Class*, 29.

[18] Veblen, *The Theory of the Leisure Class*, 29.

Cultural anthropologists Mary Douglas and Baron Isherwood, for example, argue that goods are an information system. While acknowledging that there can be a private use for goods, it is also true that

> goods are endowed with value by the agreement of fellow consumers. They come together to grade events, upholding old judgments or reversing them. Each person is a source of judgments and a subject of judgments; each individual is in the classification scheme whose discriminations he is helping to establish. By the presence of his fellows at his family funerals and weddings, by their regard for his birthdays, in their visits to his sickbed, they render marking services to him. The kind of world they create together is constructed from commodities that are chosen for their fitness to mark the events in an appropriately graded scale. Goods perish or are consumed, but this is a small part of the total consumption process. In the light of an information approach, it will seem arbitrary to define goods by the itemized market transactions that deliver them into the home. Each item can equally be perceived as a mere installment, just part of a flow of marking tape or paint that goes into the construction of a classification system. The stream of consumable goods leaves a sediment that builds up the structure of culture like coral islands. The sediment is the learned set of names and names of sets, operations to be performed upon names, a means of thinking.[19]

In light of this, it is simplistic (and condescending) to assume that members of a particular social class are incapable of making their own decisions about the nature of what they value. Moreover, Veblen and those who have taken his analysis as their own implicitly deny the moral agency of the poor. To be

---

[19] Douglas and Isherwood, *The World of Goods*, 51.

sure, power can be—and often is—exercised by one segment of society at the expense of another. However, this is not simply a matter of the wealthy oppressing the poor; different social segments are constantly interacting and seeking to affirm their own vision of life externally relative to each other and internally among their own members.

A More Virtuous Consumption

While it is not clear whether or not Lebow and Veblen are speaking prescriptively[20] or descriptively,[21] they clearly see greed and self-aggrandizement as central to a market economy. If we make their assumptions our own, we cannot help but see the pursuit of profit, wealth creation, and private property as inherently immoral. If Lebow and Veblen are correct in how the market functions, then his Holiness Patriarch Kyrill is right to worry about the "cult of consumerism."[22] If aimless production and acquisition *alone* drives the free market, then the market economy does not just exploit the moral weakness of the individual; it fundamentally deforms society. While certainly there is evidence that this can be the case, the situation is more complicated. Greed and self-aggrandizement are only two elements—albeit dark and worrying elements—in the constellation of motives and goals of a market economy. Consumerism is not intrinsic or essential to the free market but is, in fact, a deformation of it. As McCloskey points out, "Vulgar devotion to consumption alone is more characteristic

---

20 That is, greed and envy *ought* to motivate our economic decisions.

21 That is, greed and envy *do* motivate our economic decisions.

22 "Patriarch Kirill Calls to Speed Up Preparations for All-Orthodox Council," *InterFax*, March 11, 2014, http://www.interfax-religion.com/?act-news&div-11129.

of pre- and anticapitalist than of late-capitalist societies."[23] We need to balance criticism of the excesses of the market with the fact that for the tradition of the Orthodox Church, profit, wealth creation, and private property are all not only morally good but are part of God's blessing for humanity.[24]

Failing to take into account the moral goodness of wealth and the moral complexity of the market in order to criticize the cult of material prosperity or the presence of greed and envy in the marketplace can easily lead us to the opposite mistake: the facile assumption that if "more" is the problem, "less" is the solution. Doing so is to accept as real what Abba Moses calls a "fake and counterfeit coinage" that, while it has the "appearance of piety," ends up harming the poor who need (and have a right to) personal meaning and economically profitable employment, especially the poorest and most vulnerable members of the human family who cannot otherwise care for themselves.[25] The

---

[23] McCloskey, *The Bourgeois Virtues*, 24.

[24] This does not mean that we should, for example, pursue profit in immoral ways or acquire property through unjust means.

[25] It is important to note at this point that, unlike contemporary thinking, for the church fathers "the poor" are not members of an undifferentiated social class united by a lack of wealth. For example, Eric Costanzo, *Harbor for the Poor: A Missiological Analysis of Almsgiving in the View and Practice of John Chrysostom* (Eugene, OR: Pickwick, 2013), 13n14. Costanzo points out that Chrysostom makes a distinction between "beggars" (*ptōchoi*) and what today we call the working poor (*penētes*). For the latter, the church's intervention aims at autonomy and economic independence so the person can meet his or her obligations; anything that undermines human freedom, responsibility, and creativity (i.e., our ability to work) is morally wrong and must be avoided. Therefore, the entrepreneur who creates wealth and jobs is fulfilling his obligation to use his wealth on behalf of the poor (*penētes*) just as much as those who care for the *ptōchoi*. In addition, just as the wealthy are to be gener-

hard and inconvenient truth is that "you" are not necessarily any better off because "I" have less; shared material poverty is not to anyone's real advantage.

We need to avoid making the mistake Veblen does of confusing the *social function* of material goods with wealth as such. Yes, "the possession of wealth ... assumes the character of an independent and definitive basis of esteem," such that the "possession of goods, whether acquired aggressively by one's own exertion or passively by transmission through inheritance from others, becomes a conventional basis of reputability."[26] This is true within *all* segments of a society. What counts as wealth will be different for different social groups and for different cultures. At the same time, however, the *social function* of those different understandings of wealth will remain largely the same.

Anthropologically we can define wealth in terms of the relative amount of resources (e.g., time, money, and effort) needed to acquire the basic necessities of life (e.g., food, water, and shelter) as well as the range of options one has in choosing among these necessities.[27] A similar understanding of wealth

---

ous in their care for the poor, the poor (both *penētes* and *ptōchoi*) must respond with gratitude for the help they are given and are obligated to remember in prayer their benefactors whether they are the recipient of direct assistance or gainful employment. This means that even those physically incapable of work (*ptōchoi*) were expected by Chrysostom to alleviate the suffering of others. They were expected to do this not by giving money (which they did not have) but through their prayers or consoling words. Why? Because relieving the suffering of others, whether by word or deed, is a moral obligation for *all* Christians. "John exhorted the wealthy and the poor to participate" in almsgiving "as an act of virtue." Costanzo, *Harbor for the Poor*, 23, 24.

[26] Veblen, *The Theory of the Leisure Class*, 29.

[27] Douglas and Isherwood, *The World of Goods*, esp., 131–46.

leads Matt Ridley to argue that, given the shear variety of options available in a free market, all but the poorest of individuals are unimaginably wealthy relative to what was the case prior to industrialization and the rise of a market economy.[28] Accepting these gains joyfully—if cautiously—is impossible if we assume that consumption is somehow inherently sinful. If consumption is immoral, if the goal of our economic life is to consume less, then we ought to dismiss the economic gains of the last two centuries as also being immoral. Assuming this, however, reflects not only a lack of gratitude to God for his material blessings but it also condemns our neighbor to poverty.

A more virtuous model of consumption—of wealth, its creation, and use—is offered by Jeffery Tucker in a 2011 essay "In Defense of Bourgeois Civilization." He begins by asking: "Would you rather that your neighbor had a Serta© brand iComfort mattress with Cool Action Memory Foam nicely elevated above a carpeted floor in a suburban home, or that he had to sleep on a pile of straw crawling with bugs that gnawed at his flesh all night before they hid back into their nests in a dirt floor covered with layers of animal waste, in a shelter filled with soot because there is no ventilation?" Most of us would want our neighbors to have "nice, clean beds." He goes on to say that if this is what we want for our neighbor, it is also morally good to want this for our own families and ourselves. "It is not wrong," he writes, "to desire to live well."[29]

---

[28] See Matt Ridley, *The Rational Optimist: How Poverty Evolves* (New York: HarperCollins Publishers, 2010).

[29] Jeffery Tucker, "In Defense of Bourgeois Civilization," *Crisis Magazine: A Voice for the Faithful Catholic Laity*, December 27, 2011, http://www.crisismagazine.com/2011/in-defense-of-bourgeois-civilization. The words: "Would you rather that your neighbor" appear bold in the original text.

Such "a choice," however, "would not have been available to … anyone before modern times." Why? Because in the last two hundred years or so we have seen "the unleashing of creative human energy through free exchange, private ownership, and capital accumulation," which has transformed "the unimaginable poverty faced by all our ancestors into the age of plenty" for many of those born today.[30] Tucker argues that even population growth, while often seen as a problem caused by poverty, reflects the benefits of economic development.

> By modern standards, the truth is that the planet was almost unpopulated until about 1820 or so. This is not because our reproductive systems did not work. It is not because people had no interest in reproducing themselves. It is not because most of the population took vows of chastity. It is because it was hard to stay alive very long. Death ruled and life was rare. This is not love. It is, by modern standards, a living horror.[31]

Tucker's last sentence here is important when considering the totality of factors reflected in contemporary patterns of consumption in a free-market economy. Beginning "in the late Middle Ages in the Catholic countries of Europe: Spain and Italy in particular," he goes on to say that "[e]very innovation" in technology and economic development has "led to a gigantic leap forward for *life*: from horses to railroads, steam to coal, coal to oil, iron to steel, analog to digital, and onward." Yes, the presence of human sinfulness guarantees "that these inventions would sometimes be used in the service of warfare or tyranny." Tucker, however, says that even taking this into account, "the staggering majority of these inventions redounded

---

30 Tucker, "In Defense of Bourgeois Civilization."

31 Tucker, "In Defense of Bourgeois Civilization."

to the *well-being of hundreds of millions of people*," which has led to a demonstrable diminishment in

> human suffering—something the Church has always urged in the form of the Corporal Works of Mercy, and which she strives to assist. If suffering were good in itself, why would the [Roman Catholic] Church be the largest private provider of health care in the world? The result of all these inventions and advances was stark: The world population is now at 7 billion. That's seven billion wonderful lives, of equal value and sanctity to yours, dear reader—served by a global economy that is integrated and mind-bogglingly complex in every way.

Thanks to the staggering growth in the economy, "grinding poverty is no longer *imposed by material circumstances* on hundreds of millions of people.... This is the world that [political and economic] freedom made. It merits not scorn but gratitude."[32]

In a more formal way, the Russian philosopher Vladimir Solovyov made much the same point as does Tucker. Writing in *The Justification of the Good: An Essay on Moral Philosophy*,[33] Solovyov argued that "[i]f we are to give up money as an evil because many people use money for evil purposes, we ought to give up the power of ... speech, since many use it for swearing, idle talk, and slander." He goes on to say that if we give up money and the creation of wealth, then we should also "give up using fire for fear of conflagration and water for fear of persons committing suicide by drowning."[34]

---

32 Tucker, "In Defense of Bourgeois Civilization," emphasis added.

33 Vladimir Solovyov, *The Justification of the Good: An Essay in Moral Philosophy*, trans. Nathalie A. Duddington (London: Constable and Company, 1918).

34 Solovyov, *The Justification of the Good*, 359.

For Solovyov, the antidevelopment ideology that we often see (even among Christians) is an act of "unpardonable childishness."[35] As in all other areas of my life, in my economic decisions I need to be on guard against my own sinfulness. This means that I should not imagine that *my abstention* is necessarily any morally better than *your consumption*; both are tainted by sin, even as both can be a source of goodness for self and others. In addition, there is no consumption without a corresponding abstention, even as every act of abstention is in the service of an act of consumption.

The ideological rejection of development is a direct assault on what Solovyov sees as one of our primary moral obligations—the care for the poor. In a section on ascetical self-denial, he says,

> Asceticism which liberates the spirit from shameful (carnal) passions only to attach it more closely to evil (spiritual) passions is obviously a false or immoral asceticism. Its true prototype, according to the Christian idea, is the devil, who does not eat or drink and remains in celibacy. If, then, from the moral point of view we cannot approve of a wicked or a pitiless ascetic, it follows that the principle of asceticism has only a relative moral significance, namely, that it is conditioned by its connection with the principle of altruism, the root of which is pity.[36]

The love of God and love of neighbor (the latter is what Solovyov means by "altruism") is the source and goal not only of my ascetical life—of my prayer and fasting and so on—but also of my economic life. The greed and self-aggrandizement that informs consumerism are a rejection of this and should be condemned and struggled against. At the same time, we cannot do so in such a heavy-handed fashion that we lose sight of the

---

[35] Solovyov, *The Justification of the Good*, 358.

[36] Solovyov, *The Justification of the Good*, 58.

real advantages—material, social, and spiritual—of modern economic progress.

Conclusion

Human flourishing and Christian holiness require more than the mechanical pursuit of morally good goals. We must also be discerning in choosing from among the abundance of morally good goals we could theoretically pursue and the means we choose to reach those goals. This is what St. John Cassian is getting at when he quotes St. Anthony's observation that because of a lack of discernment many have fallen "prey to illusion with the result that not only could they not give a fitting end to the work they had undertaken but they brought to an abominable conclusion that high zeal of theirs and that praiseworthy mode of life."[37] The need for discernment is why, even when doing the best thing imaginable, the Virgin Mary pauses to reflect carefully and prudently on Gabriel's words. Yes, greed and self-aggrandizement can, and frequently do, inform our economic decisions. Apologists for the free market need not deny this or seek to minimize the corrupting influence of human sinfulness on our personal (or corporate) consumption. Neither should the fact of human sinfulness lead us to reject economic development as somehow being inherently sinful. Doing so is not simply wrong theologically; it is wrong practically and can lead to policies that are harmful to the poorest among us.

Finally, it is also wrong pastorally as it exempts us from our obligation to "*discern* the signs of the times" (Matt. 16:3), to bring "every thought into captivity to the obedience of Christ" (2 Cor. 10:5), and to make of our "bodies a living sacrifice" to God the Father (Rom. 12:1). What is needed instead is what the Church has always counseled: the reforming and transforming of our desires through the grace of the sacraments and ascetical struggle. It is to this that we now turn.

[37] Cassian, *Conferences*, 62.

VI Asceticism and Consumerism

The Loss of Our Original Beauty

Although we are created in the image of God, because of Adam's transgression we have lost our (personal) likeness to him. This does not mean that the fall has destroyed our humanity; the corruption of sin is *existential* not *ontological*. In other words, we ought not to think about our fallen condition as if a man had become a dog. What being a sinner does mean is that apart from grace and my own effort, I not only do bad things, I cease to be the person God created me to be. To put it more directly, I die and return to the dust from which I was taken (see Gen. 3:19; Eccl. 12:6–7).

Schmemann explains our fallen situation by asking us to think about "the Gospel account in which Christ weeps at the grave of his friend Lazarus. We need to pause and consider the meaning of these tears, for in this very moment there occurs a unique transformation within religion in relation to the long-standing religious approach to death." He goes on to say,

> Up to this moment the purpose of religion, as well as the purpose of philosophy, consisted in enabling man to come to terms with death, and if possible even to make death desirable: death as the liberation from suffering; death as freedom from this changing, busy, evil world; death as the beginning of eternity. Here, in fact, is the

> sum total of religious and philosophical teaching before Christ and outside of Christianity—in primitive religions, in Greek philosophy, in Buddhism, and so forth. But Christ *weeps* at the grave of his friend, and in so doing his own struggle with death, his refusal to acknowledge it and to come to terms with it. Suddenly, death ceases to be a normal and natural fact, it appears as something foreign, as unnatural, as fearsome and perverted, and it is acknowledged as an enemy: "The last enemy to be destroyed is death."[1]

The tragedy of our sinfulness is not only spiritual but practical, and this means that

> as we make our life an end in itself, no meaning and no goal can stand, for they are dissolved in death. It is only when we give up freely, totally, unconditionally, the self-sufficiency of our life, when we put all its meaning in Christ, that the "newness of life"—which means a new possession of the world—is given to us. The world then truly becomes the sacrament of Christ's presence, the growth of the Kingdom and of life eternal.[2]

In the liturgical tradition of the Church, to be a sinner means that I have lost my "original beauty and splendor" and now live "naked and ashamed."[3]

The universal dissonance in human experience—sickness and physical death, the often burdensome character of work, the

---

1 Alexander Schmemann, *O Death, Where Is Thy Sting?* (Crestwood, NY: St Vladimir's Seminary Press, 2003), 30.

2 Alexander Schmemann, *For the Life of the World: Sacraments and Orthodoxy* (Crestwood, NY: St Vladimir's Seminary Press, 1973), 74.

3 Ode 2, Canon of St. Andrew, http://www.saintjonah.org/services/greatcanon_sts.pdf.

presence of conflict within marriage and in society and of grief in the human heart—are all tangible symptoms of sin. In the Church's liturgical life, the consequences of sin are identified with the "garments of skins" that God fashions for Adam and Eve (Gen. 3:21). For example, on Cheesefare Sunday[4] we hear Adam's lament in the prayers for Lauds,

> "Woe is me!" Adam cried lamenting: "for the serpent and the woman have deprived me of my boldness before God, and through eating from the tree I have become an exile from the joy of Paradise. Woe is me! No more can I endure the shame. I who was once king of all God's creatures upon earth have now become a prisoner, led astray by evil counsel. I who was once clothed in the glory of immortality must now, as one condemned to die, wrap myself miserably in the skins of mortality. Woe is me! Who will share my sorrow with me? But, O Lord who lovest mankind, who hast fashioned me from the earth and art clothed in compassion, call me back from the bondage of the enemy and save me."[5]

While painful, these consequences are not motivated by malice but by the great mercy of God, serving to encourage repentance and my return to God.[6] The presence of God's mercy even in the depth of my sin is a central theme throughout Great Lent.

---

4 Cheesefare Week is the last week before Great Lent. The last Sunday before Lent is also called Forgiveness Sunday because of the rite of mutual forgiveness celebrated at Vespers on Sunday evening.

5 Mother Maria and Kallistos Ware, trans., *The Lenten Triodion* (London: Faber & Faber, 1977), 178.

6 For more on the "garments of skins," see Panayiotis Nellas, *Deification in Christ: The Nature of the Human Person*, trans., Norman Russell (Crestwood, NY: St Vladimir's Seminary Press, 1987), 43–91.

At Matins for Great and Holy Wednesday, we hear the hymn of St. Kassiani:

> The woman who had fallen into many sins recognizes Thy Godhead, O Lord. She takes upon herself the duty of a myrrh-bearer and makes ready the myrrh of mourning, before Thy entombment. Woe to me! saith she, for my night is an ecstasy of excess, gloomy and moonless, and full of sinful desire. Receive the sources of my tears, O Thou Who dost gather into clouds the water of the sea; in Thine ineffable condescension, deign to bend down Thyself to me and to the lamentations of my heart, O Thou Who didst spread out the Heavens. I will fervently embrace Thy sacred feet, and wipe them again with the tresses of the hair of my head, Thy feet at whose sound Eve hid herself for fear when she heard Thee walking in Paradise in the cool of the day. O my Saviour and soul-Saver who can trace out the multitude of my sins, and the abysses of Thy judgement? Do not disregard me Thy servant, O Thou Whose mercy is boundless.[7]

Helping people discern the presence of God's love for them even in the midst of their worst sin is at the heart of the mystery of repentance. We see this, for example, in one of the prayers of forgiveness for the sacrament of confession:

> O Lord Jesus Christ, Son of thy living God, both Shepherd and Lamb, who takest away the sins of the world ... loose, remit, forgive the sins, transgressions and iniquities, whether voluntary or involuntary, whether of wilfulness or of ignorance, which have been committed unto guilt and disobedience by these thy servants.... Master, in that thou art good and cherishest not ill-will, graciously grant unto these thy servants the word of

---

[7] George L. Papadeas, ed., *Greek Orthodox Holy Week & Easter Services* (Daytona Beach, FL: Patmos Press, 1979), 104–5.

> absolution, remitting unto them their anathema and oath, according to thy great mercy. Yea, O Lord and Master, who lovest mankind, hear thou us who make our petitions unto thy goodness on behalf of these thy servants, and disregard thou all their errors, inasmuch as thou art exceedingly merciful; and loose them from punishment eternal. For thou hast said, O Master: Whatsoever ye shall bind on earth shall be bound in heaven, and whatsoever ye shall loose on earth shall be loosed in heaven.[8]

Again, even in the depth of my sin, I can find the mercy of God. But I am getting ahead of myself.

Human Life: Natural, Individual, or Personal?

"Natural" Life: Naked and Ashamed

Because of sin, I am tempted by two equally dissonant possibilities: a "natural" life and an "individualistic" life. These terms do not have precisely the same meaning as they do in a Catholic or Protestant context. For example, "natural" does not mean for the Orthodox tradition what it means in Pope John Paul II's explication of natural law. For the late pope, "natural law"[9] seems much closer to what Orthodox Christians mean by

---

[8] Isabel Florence Hapgood, trans., *Service Book of the Holy Orthodox-Catholic Apostolic Church*, 6th ed. (Englewood, NJ: Antiochian Archdiocese of North America, 1983), 288.

[9] For example, in *Veritatis Splendor* (12) John Paul writes:

> Only God can answer the question about the good, because he is the Good. But God has already given an answer to this question: he did so *by creating man and ordering him* with wisdom and love to his final end, through the law which is inscribed in his heart (cf. Rom. 2:15), the "natural law." The latter "is nothing other than the light of understanding infused in us by God, whereby we understand what must

theosis or deification,[10] or partaking of the divine nature (see 2 Peter 1:4), than a purely secular view of human nature.[11]

---

be done and what must be avoided. God gave this light and this law to man at creation." He also did so in *the history of Israel*, particularly in the "ten words," *the commandments of Sinai*, whereby he brought into existence the people of the Covenant (cf. Ex. 24) and called them to be his "own possession among all peoples," "a holy nation" (Ex. 19:5–6), which would radiate his holiness to all peoples (cf. Wis. 18:4; Ezra 20:41). The gift of the Decalogue was a promise and sign of the *New Covenant*, in which the law would be written in a new and definitive way upon the human heart (cf. Jer. 31:31–34), replacing the law of sin which had disfigured that heart (cf. Jer. 17:1). In those days, "a new heart" would be given, for in it would dwell "a new spirit," the Spirit of God (cf. Ezra 36:24–28).

10 Fr. Dumitru Staniloae, *Orthodox Spirituality: A Practical Guide for the Faithful and a Definitive Manual for the Scholar*, trans. Archimandrite Jeromke and Otilia Kloos (Crestwood, NY: St Vladimir's Seminary Press, 2002), 363.

11 I do not think most thoughtful Orthodox Christians reject natural law as such. Rather what they reject, as the Orthodox theologian David Bentley Hart writes, is an approach to natural law that suggests that "compelling moral truths can be deduced from a scrupulous contemplation of the principles of cosmic and human nature, quite apart from special revelation, and within the context of the modern conceptual world." David Bentley Hart, "Is, Ought, and Nature's Law," *First Things*, March 2013, http://www.firstthings.com/article/2013/03/is-ought-and-natures-laws. Whether or not this is, as Hart says, "a hopeless cause," the vision of natural law he rejects is only one of many theories. In any case, contemporary Orthodox Christians have appealed to the "laws of nature and nature's God." See "A Statement of the Orthodox Christian Bishops of California in support of Proposition 8: A Constitutional

According to Staniloae, in a broad sense, *theosis* is "God's perfect and full penetration of man."[12] St. John Damascene likens *theosis* to placing iron in fire. As it is heated, the iron comes to take on the properties of fire—heat and light—while still remaining iron. In a similar fashion and beginning "at Baptism, and stretch[ing] out all along the whole of a man's spiritual ascent," the human person is gradually purified from sin and comes to acquire the virtues. "In this ascent the natural powers of man are in continual growth, and reach their apogee the moment they become capable of seeing the divine light. . . ." Thus, deification is the process through which "revival and growth is realized," and it "coincides with the . . . development of human powers to their limit, or with the full realization of human nature, but also with their unending eclipse by grace."[13]

For the tradition of the Orthodox Church a purely natural life is more akin to a life of shame, of experiencing one's humanity (and thus one's created condition), as a burden and as a source of sorrow. Or as we hear in the Canon of St. Andrew (Ode 2): "My sins have stripped me of the garment that God had woven for me, and have stitched for me robes of skin," and so now "I am clothed" in "shame as if with fig leaves" as a consequence of my "self-willed" (or self-aggrandizing) desires.

My grief and shame are symptomatic of my hedonism, of "my passions and my pleasure-loving life." The passions are described by St. Andrew as a corrupting and "heavy burden" that serve only to obscure "the beauty of my original image" created to reflect God's glory. In place of my dignity as God's creation, I have given myself over to a self-worship that serves only to adorn "the idol of my flesh with the diverse clothing of

Amendment to Restore the Definition of Marriage," http://www.antiochian.org/node/18321.

12 Staniloae, *Orthodox Spirituality*, 362.

13 Staniloae, *Orthodox Spirituality*, 363.

my shameful thoughts." Yet, sin, shame, and self-absorption are not the whole story. Although "I have buried the beauty of my original image with my passions," I still long for God: "O Savior; … seek me, as once Thou hast sought the lost coin, and find me."[14]

---

[14] Although the Orthodox understanding is markedly different from the *popular* understanding of living a natural life, I think there is some convergence between the former and how John Paul II discusses the postlapsarian experience of nakedness in his theology of the body. Reflecting on Adam's words to God after of the fall—"I heard Your voice in the garden, and I was afraid because I was naked; and I hid myself" (Gen. 3:10)—the pope observes,

> that shame, which is certainly manifested in the "sexual" order, reveals a specific difficulty in perceiving the human essentiality of one's own body. Man had not experienced this difficulty in the state of original innocence. The words, "I was afraid, because I was naked," can be understood in this way. They show clearly the consequences in the human heart of the fruit of the tree of the knowledge of good and evil.

Pope John Paul II, "A Fundamental Disquiet in All Human Existence," General Audience, May 28, 1980, http://www.ewtn.com/library/PAPALDOC/jp2tb27.htm. I think Orthodox Christians can affirm the pontiff's conclusion that Adam's words reveal "a certain constitutive break within the human person … almost a rupture of man's original spiritual and somatic unity." From this point forward, Adam "realizes for the first time that his body has ceased drawing upon the power of the spirit, which raised him to the level of the image of God." Therefore, tragically, man's "original shame bears within it the signs of a specific humiliation mediated by the body." It conceals the germ of that contradiction, which will accompany historical man in his whole earthly path, as St. Paul writes, "For I delight in the law of God according to the inward man. But I see another law in my members, warring against the law of my mind" (Rom. 7:22–23).

Individualism: Living Alone

The term *individualism*, like the term *natural*, has a different meaning for Orthodox theology than it does in popular culture. Especially in the American context,[15] we use *individual* as a synonym for "person" and *individuality* for "uniqueness." Among contemporary Orthodox theology, the Greek theologian Christos Yannaras is one of the most eloquent—if at times polemical—critics of contemporary individualism.[16] He argues that for the theological anthropology of the Orthodox Church, "'person' and 'individual' are opposite in meaning. The individual is the denial or neglect of the distinctiveness of the

---

[15] Norman Russell observes that, at least for some Orthodox Christians, "the West represents an alien ideology dominated by individualism and consumerism that threatens to overwhelm the Orthodox understanding of life as relational." Norman Russell, "'Shield of Orthodoxy' to the 'Tome of Joy': The Anti-Western Stance of Dositheos II of Jerusalem (1641–1707)," in *Orthodox Constructions of the West*, ed. George E. Demacopoulos (New York: Fordham University Press, 2013), 71.

[16] Although an important voice in Orthodox Christian ethics and theological anthropology, Yannaras is not without his critics among younger Orthodox theologians. See for example, Basilio Petrà, "Christos Yannaras and the Idea of 'Dysis,'" in *Orthodox Constructions of the West*, 161–80. Regarding our concerns here, Pantelis Kalaitzidis writes, "There is hardly a single column or essay penned by Yannaras after 1970" that does not in some way touch on what has become "his basic thesis, i.e., that the theoretical preconditions for the impasses of modern Western culture (a culture of gross consumerism) must be traced back to Western medieval theology and philosophy" (142). Pantelis Kalaitzidis, "The Image of the West in Contemporary Greek Theology," in *Orthodox Constructions of the West*, 142–60.

person."[17] As he explains, even the most "detailed descriptions … are bound to fit more than one person." We come to know each other in our uniqueness "only within the framework of direct personal relationships and communion.… Love is the supreme road to knowledge of the person, because it is an acceptance of the other person as a whole." Love, he argues, does not "project on the other person" my own "preferences, demands or desires." Rather it accepts the other as he is, "in the fullness of his uniqueness."[18] For Orthodox theology, the individual is the person who lives in isolation from his neighbor. This is not to suggest that the individual is not loved by God or that he lives a life wholly alien to love. Rather, the one who lives as an individual is the lost sheep, which the Son of Man comes to find and to save. Although fallen and living a life of estrangement from God, neighbor, and self, he is still valuable in the eyes of God and knows something of love; the individual, though alone, is not forgotten, lost to himself but not to God.[19]

---

[17] Christos Yannaras, *The Freedom of Morality*, trans. Elizabeth Briere (Crestwood, NY: St Vladimir's Seminary Press, 1984), 22.

[18] Yannaras, *The Freedom of Morality*, 23. Yannaras helps us understand how, in an individualistic culture, people will inevitably struggle with a whole range of problems related to sexuality. It is "in the self-transcendence and offering of self that is sexual love" where husband and wife learn to live in mutual acceptance of each other's uniqueness. Moreover, it is in the family (understood as an ascetical community) that children likewise learn to set aside their own sinfulness and embrace others in love. On this, see Dylan Pahman, "What Makes a Society?: An Orthodox Perspective on Asceticism, Marriage, the Family, and Society," in *Love, Marriage and Family in the Eastern Orthodox Tradition*, Sophia Studies in Orthodox Theology, vol. 7, ed. Theodore Gray Dedon and Sergey Trostyanskiy (New York: Theotokos Press, 2013), 179–93.

[19] For more on this, see the distinction between the hypostasis of ecclesial existence and the hypostasis of biological existence in

Having seen what human life is not, what does it mean to be human and what does being human mean for our economic life in a free market context?

Personal Life: Gift and Task

St. Gregory of Nyssa (335–394) made a great deal out of what he calls God's deliberation "about the best way to bring to life a creation worthy of honor" that is, humanity. Our honor and dignity are found not simply in that we are created in God's image but in the human vocation to live in his likeness. According to Fr. John Meyendorff, for St. Maximos the Confessor (580–662) "the distinction between the concepts of 'image' and 'likeness'" highlights the "polarity between" understanding our life as a "gift" and as a "task." We are created not simply to a life of "static giveness," but we are called and "challenge[d] … to *grow* in divine life." Human life is meant to be a "dynamic process" by which each human being freely responds to the invitation of divine grace to become ever more personally like God.[20] The distinction between the "'image and likeness' of God in man implies, not only an openness of man toward God, but also a *function* and *task* of man in the whole of creation."[21] Each of us is called to become united to Christ in ourselves and with the whole of creation. This is what it means to live "eucharistically" or to live a life modeled on the celebration of the Eucharist. This also means that to be who God has created me to be—to live like God—I must not only think good thoughts but do good things. Furthermore, I must do this with others because

John Zizioulas, *Being as Communion: Studies in Personhood and the Church* (Crestwood, NY: St Vladimir's Seminary Press, 1985), 49.

20 John Meyendorff, *Byzantine Theology: Historical Trends and Doctrinal Themes* (Bronx, NY: Fordham University Press, 1979), 139, emphasis in original.

21 Meyendorff, *Byzantine Theology*, 140, emphasis in original.

human flourishing, like Christian holiness, is meant to reflect the life of the Holy Trinity.

So what has all this to do with our economic life?

By providing a social context within which persons are able to create wealth, the free market can rightly be said to foster human flourishing in pursuance of the work of the Church and our personal growth in Christian holiness. While we ought not minimize the importance of wealth creation, it is important that we not lose sight of the fact that for OST it is the market's role in fostering human flourishing that provides the justification for our economic activity. Wealth is only a means to an end and that end is the dignity of the human person. While it is fair to say that by providing material resources and social space, a market economy is able to help us grow in divine life, it leaves unanswered the question of consumerism. If wealth creation is good, why not consume more to create more? Why not make consumption the goal?

Consumption and the Passionate Life

More than mere greed, consumerism is a form of idolatry; it is worshiping the works of my own hands. It is also a form of self-worship and enslavement to my own plans and projects, my own—rather than God's—vision for my life. Consumerism is a life of "self-willed desires."[22] In the ascetical theology of the Church, according to Staniloae, this reflects the presence in my life of "the passions" or those thoughts, desires, and actions that "tear [me] to pieces."[23] To live according to the passions means "to live according to the senses" in such a way that I live solely "by the senses penetrated by desire and anger" to such a degree

---

[22] Great Canon, Ode 2, http://www.saintjonah.org/services/great-canon_sts.pdf.

[23] Staniloae, *Orthodox Spirituality*, 93.

that I am "always ahead of [my]self," living not by hope but in a "fear (*Angst*)" that feeds on my "belonging to the world."[24]

The hallmark of the passionate life to Staniloae is a crippling uncertainty in the face of the possibilities that life offers. All of this is "nourished by the feeling that [man] is at the mercy of his responsibilities." I need "to forever launch out towards [some] future possibilities, ... towards [some] more appropriate opportunity." For Orthodox ascetical theology, the passions are both the cause and the symptom of enslavement to my own desires.[25]

Looking at our economic life through the lens of OST and ascetical theology helps us see that consumerism is not unique to any particular economic system. Instead, it reflects the damage sin has done to the human heart. While not necessarily an advocate of the free market, Aleksandr Solzhenitsyn helps us understand the importance of turning inward to understand the source of consumerism in the sinful human heart and thus of asceticism as the appropriate response that respects both the moral law *and* human freedom; of human life as both a gift and a task.

Cecil E. Bohanon, in his 2005 article "The Economics of Alexander Solzhenitsyn,"[26] asks, "What are the economics of Alexander Solzhenitsyn? Is Solzhenitsyn a free-market capitalist? Is he a Christian socialist? How can one characterize Solzhenitsyn's economic position?" Answering these questions "is a challenging and perhaps quixotic quest because

---

24 Staniloae, *Orthodox Spirituality*, 106.

25 Staniloae, *Orthodox Spirituality*, 116. A convenient—but by no means exhaustive—list of the passions is provided in St. Peter of Damascus, *A Treasury of Knowledge*, in *The Philokalia*, vol. 3, by G. E. H. Palmer, Philip Sherrard, and Bishop Kallistos Ware (London: Faber & Faber, 1984), 205–6.

26 Cecil E. Bohanon, "The Economics of Alexander Solzhenitsyn," *Laissez-Faire* (March-September 2005): 22–23, 35–49.

Solzhenitsyn is relatively uninterested in economic matters."[27] He concludes that

> Solzhenitsyn's approval of capitalism … is limited and less than enthusiastic. He is a continual critic of the lifestyle choices and materialism of the West. He does, however, affirm two basic institutions of a market economy: private property and free economic initiative. But even these institutions and those who participate in them must be subject to self-limitations in the spirit of Christian freedom or they will be as corrupt as their socialist counterparts.[28]

Thus, Solzhenitsyn emphasized the centrality of personal virtue for virtuous economic activity.

Joseph Pearce's 2003 interview helps us understand a bit more of Solzhenitsyn's understanding of our economic life as well. Solzhenitsyn is critical of both socialism and capitalism. Of the former he says that he has tried in "different places over the years … to prove that socialism, which to many western thinkers is a sort of kingdom of justice, was in fact full of coercion, of bureaucratic greed and corruption and avarice, and consistent within itself that socialism cannot be implemented without the aid of coercion." Unlike the Gospel which can only freely "be achieved through love, through self-limitation … socialism only uses coercion." He goes on to say, however, that "[u]ntouched by the breath of God, unrestricted by human conscience, both capitalism and socialism are repulsive."[29]

---

[27] Bohanon, "The Economics of Alexander Solzhenitsyn," 35.

[28] Bohanon, "The Economics of Alexander Solzhenitsyn," 55.

[29] Joseph Pearce, "An Interview with Alexander Solzhenitsyn," *St. Austin Review* 2, no. 2 (February 2003), http://www.catholiceducation.org/articles/arts/al0172.html.

In *The Gulag Archipelago*, Solzhenitsyn explores what it means to live a life untouched by God and lacking the restraining influence of a rightly formed conscience. He says,

> If only there were evil people somewhere insidiously committing evil deeds, and it were necessary only to separate them from the rest of us and destroy them. But the line dividing good and evil cuts through the heart of every human being. And who is willing to destroy a piece of his own heart?

He goes on to say that as we move through life,

> this line keeps changing place; sometimes it is squeezed one way by exuberant evil and sometimes it shifts to allow enough space for good to flourish. One and the same human being is, at various ages, under various circumstances, a totally different human being. At times he is close to being a devil, at times to sainthood. But his name doesn't change, and to that name we ascribe the whole lot, good and evil.

Reflecting on the opportunity to take revenge on those who have persecuted them, the prisoners "halt, stricken dumb: it is after all only because of the way things worked out that they were the executioners and we weren't." Therefore he concludes,

> From good to evil is one quaver, says the proverb. And correspondingly, from evil to good.[30]

While the immediate stakes are much less, just as the prisoners were tempted to divide their world into persecutors and the persecuted, it is so much more comforting to blame the free

30 Aleksandr I. Solzhenitsyn, *The Gulag Archipelago, 1918–1956: An Experiment in Literary Investigation*, trans. Thomas P. Whitney (Scanton, PA: Harper Collins, 1974), 168.

market (or socialism) for my own economic sins rather than looking inward at my own sinfulness.

The need for us to look inward is not meant to suggest a moral relativism between socialism and capitalism. It does however highlight the limited value of such an analysis in response to consumerism. Economic debate is so much easier and more attractive than the hard work of self-examination that Solzhenitsyn counsels. Nevertheless, an effective response to consumerism requires that we lay aside these kinds of technical economic discussions and look more closely at the ascetical dimension of our economic life.

Asceticism and Our Economic Life

Everything that we have looked at in this chapter—shame, sickness, and death—is a direct consequence of sin, that is, of my estrangement from God. It is this breakdown in the cooperative relationship between God and the human person that asceticism seeks to heal. Therefore the question is: What do I mean by asceticism?

If the passions degrade us and bind us ever more tightly to our own desires, asceticism, building on the grace of the sacraments (especially Holy Baptism and Holy Communion),[31] is those habits of thought and action that liberate us. "This is exactly the aim of asceticism: to trascend every limit, to expand souls by the audacity of love, to develop the person by means of gifts and charisms."[32] It makes possible a life progressively

---

[31] For example, Zizioulas (*Being as Communion*, 63n66) argues that "[w]ithout the ascetic dimension, the person is inconceivable. But in the end the context of the manifestation of the person is not the monastery: it is the eucharist."

[32] Paul Evdokimov, *Ages of the Spiritual Life*, trans. Michael Plekon, Alexis Vinogradov, and Sister Gertrude (Crestwood, NY: St Vladimir's Seminary Press, 1998), 187. Compare this to the descrip-

more free from sin and for obedience to God. Asceticism offers an important balance to the reductionist anthropology of the social sciences' that uncritically assume a "moral logic [that] undercuts" the possibility of community, seeing the person in terms of ever smaller "parts."[33] This need not be the case, however. Attending to our own experience, we see, as Adrian van Kaam puts it, that "differentiation takes place when" we concentrate our "attention on particular phenomena." Ideally, though, this "differentiated knowledge leads us back to a deeper, more structured knowledge of the whole." Thus, "there is no essential opposition between" a holistic, "comprehensive" view of the person and "the various differential theories," as long as in our analysis "knowledge of the whole [remains] primary."[34]

Christian asceticism has as its goal the liberation of the truly personal from the merely natural or the simply individualistic. It does this by integrating the different aspects of the human personality into a communion of love that embraces not only God and neighbor but also self and creation. In the full and proper sense, moreover, the liberty that ascetical struggle offers is not simply an absence of constraints (or negative freedom) but a "[p]erfection and sanctification" that makes possible the person's "restoration to the fullness of [his or her] existential

---

tion of asceticism in *Compendium of Catholic Social Teaching*, as the "inner transformation of the human person, in his being progressively conformed to Christ." Pontifical Council of Justice and Peace, Compendium of the Social Doctrine of the Church (Washington, DC: USCCB Publishing, 2005), 42, available online at http://www.vatican.va/roman_curia/pontifical_councils/justpeace/documents/rc_pc_justpeace_doc_20060526_compendio-dott-soc_en.html.

33 Robert N. Bellah et al., *Habits of the Heart* (Oakland: University of California Press, 1985), 144.

34 Adrian van Kaam, *Existential Foundations of Psychology* (New York: Doubleday: 1969), 116.

possibilities" and hence to be what he or she "is called to be—the *image* and *glory* of God."[35] Put slightly differently, ascetical practice and its underlying anthropology are essential to the kind of broad and deep personal freedom that makes the free market truly free. This anthropology also highlights how little freedom we might actually encounter in the market.

The Ascetical Challenge of the Free Market

Looking at the persecution of the faithful, Tertullian says that "the blood of Christians is [the] seed" of the Church.[36] Now, when Christians (at least in North America) are not violently persecuted, we find that the Church (East and West) often appears weak and frail. Should we then conclude that political and economic freedoms are inherently corrosive, that the Church can thrive in all situations except liberty? Is American culture realistically more destructive to the Church than the cruelties of the Roman, Ottoman, or Soviet empires? If not, is it rather that we have failed to discern properly the evangelical

[35] Yannaras, *Freedom of Morality*, 109, emphasis in original. In another place, Yannaras argues for the limited role of law in fostering the positive freedom of virtue. Christos Yannaras, "Existential versus Regulative Approaches: The Environmental Issue as an Existential and Not a Canonical Problem," in *Toward an Ecology of Transfiguration: Orthodox Christian Perspectives in Environment, Nature, and Creation*, ed. John Chryssavgis and Bruce V. Foltz (New York: Fordham University Press, 2013), 136–51. In the *Basis*, the Moscow Patriarchate expresses a similar idea: "The law contains a certain minimum of moral standards compulsory for all members of society. The secular law has as its task not to turn the world lying in evil into the Kingdom of God, but to prevent it from turning into hell" (4.2).

[36] Tertullian, *Apology*, 50 in *ANF* 3:55, available online at http://www.tertullian.org/anf/anf03/anf03-05.htm.

and pastoral opportunity afforded by modernity in general and the free market in particular?[37]

Living in a market economy does not require that all Christians become monks, but it does require an ascetical response. This is especially so when we are facing the challenge of consumerism, which severs the organic link between person and community. If political totalitarianism does this at the expense of the person, consumerism does it at the expense of the community. The irony is that, in both cases, we are less than we should be as both persons and a community. Human flourishing requires that we find the balance between personal uniqueness and communal life. Flourishing, to say nothing of Christian holiness, requires that we give ourselves away freely in love. Such love is impossible if, as the eighteenth century Irish statesman Edmund Burke reminds us, we have not placed "a controlling power upon will and appetite." He goes on to say that

> the less of it there is within, the more there must be without. It is ordained in the eternal constitution of things, that men of intemperate minds cannot be free. Their passions forge their fetters.[38]

What Burke is pointing to here is, in the Orthodox Church, the goal of ascetical struggle. Asceticism is the practical means by which we break the fetters that bind us.

---

[37] This material is drawn, in part, from an essay I wrote for *Ethika Politika*. See Gregory Jensen, "The Forgotten Good of American Individualism," *Ethika Politika*, May 20, 2014, http://ethikapolitika.org/2014/05/20/forgotten-good-american-individualism/.

[38] Edmund Burke, "Letter to a Member of the National Assembly, in Answer to Some Objections to His Book on French Affairs," in *The Works of the Right Honourable Edmund Burke*, vol. 4 (London: John C. Nimmo, 1887), 52, quoted in Pahman, "What Makes a Society?" 190 (see n. 18).

George F. Will, in a December 2012 speech delivered at Washington University in St. Louis, observed that "ancients had asked what is the highest of which mankind is capable and how can we pursue this? Hobbes and subsequent modernists asked: What is the worst that can happen and how can we avoid it?"[39] Christian asceticism, rooted as it is in a holistic understanding of the human person and the human condition, answers both these questions by reminding us in very practical ways (e.g., fasting, sexual restraint, the importance of prayer, manual labor, and care for the poor) that we cannot be our best unless we are first able to prevent ourselves from being our worst. As we will see in the next chapter, this is precisely what is embodied in the ascetical practice of the Orthodox Church.

[39] George F. Will, "Religion and Politics in the First Modern Nation," originally presented at Washington University in St. Louis, December 4, 2012, in *Renewing the American Constitutional Tradition*, ed. Peter Berkowitz (Stanford: Hoover Institutional Press, 2013), 129–43, http://www.hoover.org/news/read-renewing-american-constitutional-tradition-new-collection-hoover-institution-press.

VII Shaping Desire

It is through our personal asceticism that we are able to develop a way of life that helps us avoid the excesses in our economic life that slowly (and sometimes not so slowly) tear us to pieces. Just as Christ transforms an "instrument of death into a source of life,"[1] ascetical struggle transforms mere consumption into an event of communion. Archimandrite Vasileios offers us some insight into how this transformation occurs. He writes,

> The world in which man lives according to his nature as a theanthropic entity is the liturgical world. It is not time as represented by history, nor space as represented by creation, nor the logic of fallen man, nor the skill of the unstable individual. Within the Liturgy everything has been changed for the better, tested—that is, broken and restored—through the Cross and Resurrection.[2]

---

1 Canticle Seven, Matins for Sunday of the Veneration of the Holy Cross, http://www.fordham.edu/Halsall/basis/triodion/lent3sun.txt.

2 Archimandrite Vasileios of Stavronikita, *Hymn of Entry: Liturgy and Life in the Orthodox Church*, trans. Elizabeth Briere (Crestwood, NY: St Vladimir's Seminary Press, 1984), 67.

Building on the grace poured out in the sacraments, the ascetical disciplines of prayer, fasting, manual labor, almsgiving and the monastic vows of poverty, chastity, obedience, and stability are the practical means that break and restore our consumption, and indeed the whole of life (including its economic dimension) to the service of communion.[3]

Because our conversation is focused on economics rather than the spiritual life as such, our consideration of the ascetical disciplines and the vows foundational to the monastic life will unfortunately be very brief. Actually it would be fair to say that what follows is impressionistic and is in no way anything more than the barest introduction to topics that, were they to be discussed in any depth, would take us far afield. Nevertheless, having looked at consumerism through the lens of the Church's ascetical tradition, I think it would be helpful to have at least a glimpse of the disciplines at the heart of the Orthodox Church's understanding of the spiritual life.

Both in the interest of time and for analytical purposes, we will look at the ascetical disciplines in pairs: prayer and fasting and almsgiving and manual labor. We will likewise look at the monastic vows in pairs: poverty and chastity and obedience

---

[3] While most of us are not called to monastic life, Florovsky is right when he says that "the monastic ideal" of personal "union with God through prayer, through humility, through obedience, through constant recognition of one's sins, voluntary or involuntary, through a renunciation of the values of this world, through poverty, through chastity, through love for mankind and love for God" summarizes the Orthodox understanding of the life of Christian discipleship. Fr. George Florovsky, "The Ascetic Ideal and the New Testament," in *The Collected Works of Georges Florovsky*, vol. 10: *The Byzantine Ascetic and Spiritual Fathers* (Vaduz, Germany: Buchervertriebsanstalt, 1987), 17. This means that some form of what we might deem "monastic practices" are at the heart of all Christian life and so our life of personal asceticism.

and stability. Hopefully this will help us see ascetical struggle and the monastic life not merely as "rules for behavior and the evaluation of individual character" rooted in authority or convention and accepted "on utilitarian grounds" but for what they are: "the dynamic response of personal freedom" in response to divine grace by which we are saved.[4]

The Ascetical Disciplines

Prayer and Fasting

One of the most common observations made about the ascetical (and, for that matter, liturgical) tradition of the Orthodox Church is that it is *physically* demanding. More than one visitor has come up to me after Vespers on Saturday evening or Divine Liturgy on Sunday and commented that they thought the service was lovely but they were so tired from standing the whole time.[5] We are bodily creatures and, even though damaged by sin (i.e., sickness and death), Christos Yannaras reminds us that the "material body partakes in the perfection of man, in his sanctification." Because salvation "involves man's being as a whole," both body and soul need to be redirected toward the proper end of human life: communion with God.[6]

This is why our first pairing is prayer and fasting. "Prayer," says the monk and ascetic Evagrius of Pontus (345–399), "is a conversation of the spirit with God." A life of prayer requires that we form within ourselves "the disposition that the spirit needs … to be able to reach out towards its Lord and to hold

---

4 Christos Yannaras, *The Freedom of Morality*, Contemporary Greek Theologians, no. 3 (Yonkers, NY: St Vladimir's Press, 2003), 14–15.

5 Great Vespers on Saturday night is never less than forty-five minutes and depending on the feast can easily go for an hour or a bit more; Sunday Divine Liturgy typically lasts ninety minutes to two hours.

6 Yannaras, *Freedom of Morality*, 109.

converse with him without any intermediary." According to St. Maximus the Confessor the material world as such is not an obstacle to this conversation. "It is not food that is evil, but gluttony … not material things but avarice.… [I]t is only the misuse of things that is evil, and such misuse occurs when the intellect fails to cultivate its natural powers."[7]

In order to craft an anthropologically and economically sound response to consumerism, we need to understand the psychology of the passions, of how the heart's desires and the needs of the body hinder the soul's ascent to God. There is a sequence to the development of the passions. First there is the image, then the thought about the image. The thought moves me to action and from repeated action comes the habit of misuse or the passion. What needs to be broken is the connection between the mental image and my thoughts about it. This is where prayer becomes existentially liberating.

Over time, prayer reforms and transform how I think about God and his creation. In addition to being physical,[8] Orthodox prayer is also poetic. The services of the Church offer us multiple images about, well, just about everything. Liturgical prayer especially offers us a syntax for human life (from conception through natural death to the life to come), for the whole created order (seen and unseen), and for the life of the Holy Trinity. The liturgical prayer of the Church corrects the passions by

---

7 St. Maximos the Confessor, "Four Hundred Texts on Love," 3.4 in *The Philokalia* by St. Nicodemus of the Holy Mountain and St. Makarios of Corinth, vol. 2, trans., G. E. H. Palmer, Philip Sherrard, and Kallistos Ware (London: Faber and Faber, 1981), 83.

8 In addition to standing, Orthodox Christians will make deep bows and prostrations in the ordinary course of liturgical and personal prayer.

slowly reforming our egocentric thoughts so that we come to see creation as God sees it.[9]

Logically, prayer has the priority in our ascetical life because it heals the passions at their source—the human heart. Given that we are physical creatures, we typically need to begin with external bodily disciplines and seek to overcome the passions moving from the outside in. We need to develop new habits and allow these new habits of action (the virtues) to reform our habits of thinking. This is where fasting helps me learn to deny my tendency to engage the world in an egocentric manner. My "bodily knowledge" of sin and death are gradually displaced as I come to "bodily knowledge" of God. "If you want your heart to become a place for the mysteries of the world" of grace, writes St. Isaac the Syrian (c. 613–c. 700), "first become rich in corporeal works: in fasting, vigils, service, asceticism, patience, the destruction of troublesome thoughts and the rest" (*Letter* 4).[10]

Almsgiving and Manual Labor

Through prayer and fasting I reshape my heart and make it more sensitive and responsive to God's grace. The ascetical disciplines of manual labor and almsgiving allow me to shape the world around me and my relationship with others—including the poor—in a manner that reflects Christ. Just as prayer and fasting sanctify soul and body, almsgiving and manual labor are the means by which I sanctify the material world and

---

[9] This distinction is important. God is not simply one object among others—albeit the best and most perfect—he is rather the light by which we see light itself (see Ps. 36:9). For more on the transformation of human knowing, see Michael E. Butler, "Perception of the *Logoi* and Cure of the Soul in St. Maximus the Confessor," *Edification: The Transdisciplinary Journal of Christian Psychology* 6, no. 2 (2012): 114–24.

[10] Quoted in Yannaras, *Freedom of Morality*, 117.

therefore human society as well. This dual sanctification reflects the fact that because we are bodily creatures we are also social and traditional creatures. Fidelity to God's grace and our own deepest identity has implications for how we use the material creation as well as how we structure the various groups and communities that comprise our social world. Just as wheat and grapes become in turn bread and wine and then the body and blood of Christ, so our social world must be formed, reformed, and transformed into an ever more faithful icon of the kingdom (cf. Col. 2:17; Heb. 8:5; 10:1). Not only must I love God with all my heart and all my soul and all my strength, I must also love my neighbor as myself (cf. Matt. 22:37–39; Luke 10:27; Mark 12:30; cf. Deut. 6:5). However, I cannot credibly claim to love my neighbor if I am indifferent to society in which he and I live together (cf. 1 John 4:20–21).[11]

After the New Testament period, one of the most vivid illustrations of the convergence of almsgiving and manual labor

---

[11] Therefore the

> Church also calls her faithful children to participation in the life of society, which should be based on the principles of Christian morality. In the High Priestly Prayer, the Lord Jesus interceded the Heavenly Father for His followers: "I pray not that thou shouldest take them out of the world, but that thou shouldest keep them from the evil [one].... As thou hast sent me into the world, even so have I also sent them into the world" (John 17:15, 18). It is inadmissible to shun the surrounding world in a Manichean way. Christian participation in it should be based on the awareness that the world, socium and state are objects of God's love, for they are to be transformed and purified on the principles of God-commanded love. The Christian should view the world and society in the light of his ultimate destiny, in the eschatological light of the Kingdom of God. (*Basis* 1.3).

is found among the first monks in the Egyptian deserts. The desert fathers would often live in places where they had access to palm leaves. The monks would weave them into mats and baskets while they prayed, then sell their handiwork to support themselves. Whatever was not needed to meet their own, minimal expenses would be given to the poor.

Like all the passions, consumerism alienates me from the world of persons, events, and things. In its grip my relationship not only to the world around me but also to God and myself becomes characterized by anxiety. Although his concerns were different from ours here, St. Simeon the New Theologian (949–1002) tells why this is so when he writes that "the mind is something that is in constant motion and incapable of total inactivity." For this reason "it is necessary that it should be concerned with and eager to practice the commandments of God." Unfortunately, because the passions keep me from eager obedience, my life "is filled with care and concern." Although I imagine that with this or that next purchase it will be otherwise, I "cannot be wholly at leisure." "But in the beginning," says Simeon, it was not this way: "Adam was enjoined to till the ground and care for it [cf. Gen. 2:15] and there is in us a natural bent for work, the movement toward the good. Those who yield themselves to idleness and apathy, even though they may be spiritual and holy, hurl themselves into unnatural subjection to passions."[12]

St. Basil the Great (329–379) in *The Long Rule* stresses the importance of work to our spiritual life. He tells his monastic brothers (and us) that they (and we), "must toil with diligence and not think that our goal of piety offers an escape from work or a pretext for idleness, but occasion for struggle, for ever greater

---

[12] Symeon the New Theologian, *Catechesis*, 10.3 in idem, *Symeon the New Theologian: The Discourses*, trans., C. J. De Catanzaro (New York: Paulist Press, 1980), 164.

endeavor, and for patience in tribulation."[13] Work is not only "beneficial for bringing the body into subjection, but also for showing charity to our neighbor in order that through us God may grant sufficiency to the weak among our brethren."

The philanthropic end of work is something that the Church has known from its earliest days. St. Basil cites the example of the apostle Paul:

> Yes, you yourselves know that these hands have provided for my necessities, and for those who were with me. I have shown you in every way, by laboring like this, that you must support the weak (Acts 20:34–35).

Again citing the example of Paul, Basil says that our labor is not simply for ourselves but also so that we "may have something to give him who has need" (Eph. 4:28).

Labor for Basil is not only important ascetically and philanthropically but also soteriologically and eschatologically. Speaking of the former, St. Basil says,

> [I]n the midst of our work can we fulfill the duty of prayer, giving thanks to him who has granted strength to our hands for performing our tasks and cleverness to our minds for acquiring knowledge, and for having provided the materials, for that which is in the instruments we use and that which forms the matters of the art in which we may be engaged, praying that the work of our hands may be directed toward its goal, the good pleasure of God.[14]

Through our labor, we can "acquire a recollected spirit" (peace and wholeness of being) if we combine it with prayer, asking

---

[13] St. Basil, *Ascetical Works*, trans. M. Monica Wagner, C.S.C., *The Fathers of the Church: A New Translation*, vol. 9 (Washington, DC: The Catholic University Press, 1950), 306.

[14] Basil, *Ascetical Works*, 308.

"in every action" that God bring success to "our labors." In this way, "we satisfy our debt of gratitude to Him who gave us the power to do the work, and when, as has been said, we keep before our minds the aim of pleasing Him."[15] Consonant with the Church's holistic understanding of salvation, human work is meant to unite thanksgiving to God, wealth creation, and human flourishing. This holistic understanding of work is what I mean when I say consumption is for production. Likewise it is this catholic view of work that we lose sight of when production is meant for mere consumption.

The soteriological and eschatological dimension that work offers is the strongest ascetical correction to consumerism. Again from *The Long Rule*:

> Thus we may be accounted worthy to hear the words: "Come ye blessed of my Father, possess you the kingdom prepared for you from the foundation of the world. For I was hungry and you gave me to eat; I was thirsty and you gave me to drink."[16]

The tradition of the Church never denies the utilitarian or practical value of human work. In fact, given the moral imperative to care for others, the wealth creating potential of work is not only assumed but baptized. We will come back to the relationship between work and philanthropy in a moment. For now, though, it is important to emphasize that within the tradition of the Church, the ascetical value of labor is associated specifically with *manual* labor.

St. John Chrysostom makes this very point when in a homily on St. Paul's first epistle to the Church at Corinth he tells his listeners,

---

15 Basil, *Ascetical Works*, 308.

16 Basil, *Ascetical Works*, 307.

> Whensoever then thou seest one driving nails, smiting with a hammer, covered with soot, do not therefore hold him cheap, but rather for that reason admire him. Since even Peter girded himself, and handled the drag-net, and went fishing after the Resurrection of the Lord.[17]

St. Augustine (354–430) also recommends manual labor. In "Of the Work of Monks," he says St. Paul "did bodily work, and thereby lived in the flesh, and did not use the power which the Lord had given to the Apostles, that preaching the Gospel he should live by the Gospel, those things above-said do without all doubt bear witness." As for "what sort of work he did, or when he did it," the bishop of Hippo is uncertain. One thing he does know is that Paul did not "steal, nor was a housebreaker or highwayman, nor chariot-driver or hunter or player, nor given to filthy lucre." The apostolic witness is one that "innocently and honestly wrought things which are fitted for the uses of men; such as are the works of carpenters, builders, shoemakers, peasants, and such like." He goes on to say,

> [T]he Apostle then would not disdain either to take in hand any work of peasants, or to be employed in the labor of craftsmen. For he who says, Be without offense to Jews and to Greeks and to the Church of God, before what men he could possibly stand abashed, I know not. If they shall say, the Jews; the Patriarchs fed cattle: if the Greeks, whom we call also Pagans; they have had philosophers, held in high honor, who were shoemakers: if the Church of God; that just man, elect to the testimony of a conjugal

[17] St. John Chrysostom, "On First Corinthians," in *NPNF*[1] 11:117 (ed. Phillip Schaff; Peabody, MA: Hendrickson, 1996). Although we cannot explore the matter here as it would take us too far afield, it is important to note that Chrysostom's reference to the apostle Peter and St. Basil's to the apostle Paul suggests that manual labor has an *evangelical* dimension.

> and ever-during virginity, to whom was betrothed the Virgin Mary who bore Christ, was a carpenter.

And so he concludes that any work done innocently and "without fraud ... is good."[18]

Physical labor, work that I do with my own hands, allows me to shape the material world directly. This is not to denigrate or minimize intellectual work. Much less is this to recommend an antitechnological attitude. It is however to say that we are physical creatures, and so for this reason it is important that we all engage in some type of manual labor. To those the fathers list, we can add cooking, cleaning, sewing, gardening, automobile repair, plumbing, or any other forms of physical work, whether done for pay or not.

The fathers do not just recommend work; they tie it to almsgiving. After meeting my obligations to my family, this means caring for the poor. I do not work just for myself but for others—for their flourishing and even for their sanctification. We have seen this connection between work and our social life in the desert fathers as well as in the later fathers—in particular Basil, Chrysostom, and Augustine. Together the lesson from Scripture and the fathers is that manual labor and almsgiving help me give a Christlike form both to my personal life as well as to society.

Monastic Vows

When we looked at asceticism in general, our discussion was brief as will be our discussion of monastic life. We will look at the monastic vows in the pairs of poverty and chastity and

---

[18] St. Augustine, "Of the Works of Monks," 14 in *NPNF*[1] 3:511.

obedience and stability to help us understand how to reshape the desires that inform our economic decisions.[19]

For some, the monastic emphasis in Orthodox spirituality seems strange, exotic, and even foreign. Yet as Florovsky writes, "the monastic ideal," as he calls it, of "union with God through prayer, through humility, through obedience, through constant recognition of one's sins, voluntary or involuntary, through a renunciation of the values of this world, through poverty, through chastity, through love for mankind and love for God,"[20] simply *is* the Christian life. While monastic life is not "the only path, not ... the path for everyone," it is nevertheless a "fully authentic path of Christian life."[21] For the Tradition of the Church it is in

[19] Metropolitan Hilarion, in the "Importance of Monasticism," writes: "This yoke of Christ is expressed most clearly in the following vows pronounced by a person in the face of the Church before he or she assumes 'the angelic image':

- to stay in a monastery and hold fast until the last breath [i.e., stability];
- to preserve oneself in virginity, chastity and reverence [i.e., chastity];
- to obey the abbot and all the brethren in Christ [i.e., obedience];
- to remain until death in non-possession and voluntary poverty in coenobitic life for the sake of Christ [i.e., poverty];
- to accept all the rules of monastic life, the rules of holy fathers and orders of the abbot;
- to be ready to endure every inconvenience and sorrow of the monastic life for the sake of the Heavenly Kingdom."

The vows clearly presuppose each other and interpenetrate. For simplicity sake, I have summarized them as poverty, chastity, obedience, and stability.

[20] Florovsky, "Ascetic Ideal and the New Testament," 17.

[21] Florovsky, "Ascetic Ideal and the New Testament," 18.

the "monastic ideal" that we see most clearly the possibility for all Christians "to attain a creative spiritual freedom ... in God the Father, God the Son, and God the Holy Spirit." It is in monastic life that we see that "the path to becoming free, the path in which humanity fully becomes human precisely because the created existence of humanity is contingent upon God, [which] is by itself bordered on both sides by non-existence" is possible only through radical obedience to God. The central witness of monastic life is the assertion "that to become a slave to God is ontologically and existentially the path to becoming free."[22]

Poverty and Chastity

St. John Climacus, in *The Ladder of Divine Ascent*, describes monastic poverty as "the resignation of cares." Having embraced poverty the monk is able to live a "life without anxiety" and undertake the spiritual life as an "unencumbered traveler," free "from sorrow" and faithful "to the commandments."[23] Without minimizing the material aspects of poverty, the saint emphasizes its inner meaning. Through poverty the monk is "journeying to heaven,"[24] but only because he has "entrusted his cares to God"[25] and with "unwavering faith cuts off" the transient cares of this life in "remembrance of death" and of the judgment that is to come.[26] To understand what poverty is, and more importantly what it is not, we need to look not at what Climacus says about poverty but the vice it is meant to cure: avarice.

---

22 Florovsky, "Ascetic Ideal and the New Testament," 17.

23 John Climacus, *John Climacus: The Ladder of Divine Ascent*, trans. Archimandrite Lazarus Moore (New York: Harper & Brothers, 1959), 17.1.

24 Climacus, *The Ladder*, 17.16.

25 Climacus, *The Ladder*, 17.2.

26 Climacus, *The Ladder*, 17.12.

According to Climacus, the greedy and avaricious person is an idolater who "prays to material images" while the man who is free of avarice "is pure during prayer."[27] Just as waves "never leave the sea," neither "do anger and grief leave the avaricious."[28] Seemingly for Climacus, there is not a personal sin or a social harm that does not trace its origin to avarice: "The love of money is (and is called) the root of all evil [1 Tim. 6:10] because it produces hatred, thefts, envy, separations, enmities, storms, remembrance of wrong, hard-heartedness, murders."[29] Finally, while the heart that is detached from material goods is free from "quarrels and controversies … the covetous man will fight till death for a needle."[30]

Especially when talking about those who are not called by God to be monks or nuns, it is important that we not confuse poverty with the mere absence of material possessions or equate it with annual income. To do so is to afflict ourselves and others with what Climacus calls "a double harm." The man "who impoverishes himself for no reason," he says, suffers the loss of the "present goods" of this life while at the same time depriving himself of "future ones" in the life to come.[31]

Even for monastics, the renunciation of personal property (the ascetical and canonical heart of the vow) does not translate necessarily to the absence of wealth: "In Christian history," the *Basis* says,

> many communities would pool property, abandoning personal proprietary aspirations. This kind of property relations contributed to the consolidation of the spiritual

[27] Climacus, *The Ladder*, 17.4.

[28] Climacus, *The Ladder*, 17.10.

[29] Climacus, *The Ladder*, 17.11.

[30] Climacus, *The Ladder*, 17.11.

[31] Climacus, *The Ladder*, 17.7.

> unity of the faithful and in many cases proved rather effective economically, as in the case of Orthodox monasteries. **However, the repudiation of private property in the early apostolic community (Acts 4:32) and later in coenobite monasteries was exclusively a voluntary affair and a personal spiritual option.** (*Basis*, 7.3, emphasis in original)[32]

Poverty as a virtue, then, is less a matter of what I own and more of my attitude toward my possessions and how I use them. The inner meaning of poverty is simplicity of life. Such simplicity

---

[32] Wealthy communities, like wealthy Christians, have existed from the earliest days of monasticism. Maintaining, increasing, and securing the use of wealth in ways that foster rather than hinder the vocation of the monks likewise has also been a concern from almost the beginning. See, for example, *Byzantine Monastic Foundation Documents: A Complete Translation of the Surviving Founders' Typika and Testaments,* ed. John Thomas and Angela Constantinides Hero (Washington, DC: Dumbarton Oaks, 2000), 43, http://www.doaks.org/resources/publications/doaks-online-publications/byzantine-monastic-foundation-documents. They write,

> Since monasticism itself had its origins in Egypt in the fourth century as a movement of lay piety, the first monasteries were themselves necessarily private foundations. Although the emperors and the ecclesiastical hierarchy sponsored churches from the time of Constantine (306–337), there was at first no tradition of patronage of monasteries by the public authorities of late antiquity. Many bishops who did later found monasteries, beginning in the fifth century, chose to regard them as personal possessions rather than as diocesan institutions. So even before the end of late antiquity, the tradition of the Byzantine monastery's independence of public authority had struck deep roots.

I hope in a later work on property rights in OST to examine the canonical status of monastic property.

is not only material but also holistic: emotional, social, and spiritual. Whether in monastic life or not, the goal of simplicity is poverty of spirit (Matt. 5:3) and purity of heart (5:8). This brings us to the second of our monastic virtues: chastity.

Although often overlooked today, St. Paul encourages all Christians to remain unmarried. Like St. John Climacus' discussion of poverty, the apostle counsels celibacy in the service of both practical and spiritual freedom: "But I want you to be without care. He who is unmarried cares for the things of the Lord—how he may please the Lord. But he who is married cares about the things of the world—how he may please his wife" (1 Cor. 7:32–33). Nevertheless, just as not all Christians are called to material poverty, not all Christians are called to celibacy. "[E]ach one has his own gift from God, one in this manner and another in that.... [A]s God has distributed to each one, as the Lord has called each one, so let him walk" (7:7, 17). Akin to poverty, the key to chastity is not whether the person is married or not. Rather, within the tradition of the Church the virtue "of chastity ... is the basis of the inner unity of the human personality, which should always be in the state of harmony between its mental and bodily powers" (*Basis*, 10.6). Sin, such as fornication and adultery, "inevitably ruins the harmony and integrity of one's life, damaging heavily one's spiritual health." Likewise, the absence of chastity "dulls the spiritual vision and hardens the heart, making it incapable of true love." While the synod fathers are speaking here of sexual morality, it is not much of a leap to see that the same vices that make the "happiness of full-blooded family life ... unattainable" also foster consumerism and disrupt the virtuous functioning of the economic order. "Sins against chastity," they write,

> also lead to negative social consequences. In the situation of a spiritual crisis of the human society, the mass media and the products of the so-called mass culture sometimes become instruments of moral corruption by praising

> sexual laxity, all kinds of sexual perversion and other sinful passions. Pornography, which is the exploitation of the sexual drive for commercial, political or ideological purposes, contributes to the suppression of the spiritual and moral principles, thus reducing man to an animal motivated by instinct alone. (*Basis*, 10.6)

Avarice and sexual immorality both result in unwholesome forms of consumption that hinder rather than foster human flourishing and Christlike holiness. With only minor changes, the synod fathers' condemnation of "pornography and fornication" are equally applicable to avarice. Just as "the Church does not at all call to abhor the body or sexual intimacy as such," it does not condemn wealth or property. Instead, in the sexual and economic aspects of our lives, what is rejected is "the tendency to turn chaste and appropriate relations"—and economic activity—"as God has designed them" into occasions "of humiliating exploitation," characterized by "egoistic, impersonal, loveless and perverted pleasure" that is "completely divorced from personal and spiritual communion, selflessness and all-round responsibility" for my neighbor (*Basis*, 10.6).

Obedience and Stability

"Great is he who piously renounces possessions," says St. John Climacus, "but holy is he who renounces his will. The one will receive a hundredfold, either in money or in graces, but the other will inherit eternal life."[33] Poverty—or maybe more broadly, simplicity—is, like chastity, not only laudable but also essential to human flourishing, to say nothing of the Christian life. However, without obedience to the divine will neither poverty nor chastity is of any value.

---

[33] Climacus, *The Ladder*, 17.9.

As the etymology of the word suggests (from Latin *obedire*, *oboedire*—literally to hear or listen), obedience is more than merely doing what I am told (what Paul in Ephesians 6:6 calls "eyeservice"). Obedience is a prayerful or contemplative attention to God that leads to right action. The heart of obedience is discernment, a virtue that in turns flows from the "fountain of … humility."[34] St. John Climacus says that for beginners in the spiritual life, discernment takes the form of accurate self-knowledge that in time matures into "a spiritual sense that faultlessly distinguishes what is truly good from what is of nature and opposed to it." In its fullness, discernment is divinely revealed "knowledge … which can enlighten with its lamp what is dark in others." Or more simply and directly: "discernment is, and is recognized as, the assured understanding of the divine will on all occasions, in every place and in all matters; and it is only found in those who are pure in heart, and in body and in mouth."[35]

The saint goes on to emphasize not only the practical side of discernment but also its vocational dimension:

> We must use great discernment in order to know when to take our stand against sin, and in what cases and to what extent to struggle against the food of the passions, and when to withdraw from the fray. For, on account of our weakness, sometimes it is necessary to acknowledge that flight is better than death.[36]

Obedience, like discernment, is at the service of vocational fidelity (stability). Discerning and obedient consumption or use of the material world as well as my participation in the market should be guided by, and in support of, my personal vocation.

[34] Climacus, *The Ladder*, 25.69.

[35] Climacus, *The Ladder*, 26.1.

[36] Climacus, *The Ladder*, 26.183.

Although I admire monastic life, I am not a monk. This means more than simply that I am married. It also means that I have moral and practical obligations that the monk in his monastery does not have or, at least, not in the same way that I do.

The point here (and this returns us to the story of the two monks from the introduction) is that while we can exclude some things as immoral—things we ought not to do—the good that we should do is dependent on a broad range of factors. These include not only circumstances and resources but also the vocation or the calling of the actor. It is here, in the vocation of the person that we can locate the cause and cure of the passion of consumerism.

St. Antony the Great says that if I would know God, I must first know myself. I would add that self-knowledge also requires self-acceptance, though not passivity in the face of sinfulness. Self-acceptance must reflect my willingness to admit that I am a sinner and to struggle against my own sinfulness (repentance). Just as repentance requires that I accept my sinfulness, growth in virtue requires that I learn to become more fully the person God has called me to be within the concrete circumstances of my life. This means that self-knowledge and wholesome self-acceptance require appropriate self-expression, and all this in Christ.

In the final analysis, consumerism is not so much an economic failure as it is a vocational failure. Monastic fidelity reminds me that my economic life needs to reflect not mere desire but obedience to my own personal calling. The proper response to consumerism is not less consumption but better spiritual formation. According to Christ, ascetical self-denial, though essential, is insufficient:

> When an unclean spirit goes out of a man, he goes through dry places, seeking rest, and finds none. Then he says, "I will return to my house from which I came." And when he comes, he finds it empty, swept, and put

> in order. Then he goes and takes with him seven other spirits more wicked than himself, and they enter and dwell there; and the last state of that man is worse than the first. So shall it also be with this wicked generation. (Matt. 12:43–45)

The moral challenge of consumerism, and for that matter of the market economy, is one answered not by power and control but, as Conyer writes, "on the right relation of things in a world that both begins and ends in mystery."[37] Absent the living sense of vocation that spiritual formation discovers and fosters, we are left with a life that "is no more or less than the kaleidoscope patterns of … individuals," who "freely" consume the good things of creation while at the same time, ironically and tragically, "struggle to escape" the consequences of their choices.[38]

---

[37] A. J. Conyer, *The Listening Heart: Vocation and the Crisis of Modern Culture* (Dallas: Spence Publishing, 2006), 79. He goes on to say that the modern era's

> adulation of power and mastery, and the promotion of power as an end in itself … began in certain theological issues that become for later times a sort of template for understanding the nature of power. Could God do anything on the basis of his *potential absoluta*, or was he in fact limited by his attributes of goodness, love, patience, humility and so on? Does his character in other words, grow out of his power? Or is his power an expression of his character? (93–94)

See as well, John Milbank, "Suspending the Material: The Turn of Radical Orthodoxy," in *Radical Orthodoxy: A New Theology*, ed. John Milbank, Catherine Pickstock, and Graham Ward (London: Routledge, 1999).

[38] See A. J. Conyer, *The Listening Heart*, 104.

Conclusion

The tradition of the Church offers us a better way. To see this better way (not to mention to *live* it), it is important to keep in mind, as Yannaras puts it, that "to be *saved* means" that the person "becomes 'safe and *sound*,' or *whole*, and realizes to the full his potential for existence and life beyond space, time and conventional relationships." To return to language we have used throughout, we can say that to be saved encompasses not only Christian holiness but also human flourishing. If to be saved "means conquering death," it is a victory that embraces being both a saint and a wholesome human being. I must not only be a good Christian but also a good man.[39]

Anthropologically, Yannaras continues, this reflects the "insatiable thirst" that is "common" to each of us for "*salvation*," not just for "conventional improvements in character or behavior." The ascetical tradition of the Church reveals the "truth of man,"[40] concerning which I am "capable of either accepting or rejecting." This means that in my economic dealings, I "can refuse the freedom of love and personal communion." That refusal is consumerism. I "can say 'no' to God and cut [myself] off" from him in how I choose to consume the things of creation, or I can choose instead to enter into a "personal *relationship* with God."[41] To choose the latter is to choose to live a life of communion with God that reveals my own personal "distinctiveness," "within [a] framework of ... personal intimacy" that in turn makes it possible for me to accept you as you are "in the fullness" of your own "personal uniqueness."[42]

---

39 Yannaras, *Freedom of Morality*, 15.

40 Yannaras, *Freedom of Morality*, 16.

41 Yannaras, *Freedom of Morality*, 20, emphasis in original.

42 Yannaras, *Freedom of Morality*, 21.

Thus, if consumerism requires an ascetical response, this response must be the fruit of the spiritual formation of the person, of that process by which the person comes to discover and incarnate his personal vocation.[43]

[43] I am indebted to the late Fr. Richard D. Byrne, OCSO, who describes spiritual formation as the discovery and incarnation of one's own deepest identity in Christ. May his memory be eternal.

VIII Conclusion

Take Captive Every Thought

The Freedom of the Free Market

The free market is not a formal social institution like the Church or a more informal institution like family. Nor is the free market a physical space like a grocery store, a shopping mall, or the markets that grew up around medieval monasteries. The term *free market* is a construct, a handy way of talking about the myriad economic decisions that all of us make every day.

We use this linguistic shortcut because the only thing more diverse than *what* we exchange and the social situations in which these exchanges are made are the many different—and often conflicting—motivations for *why* we make these exchanges. The motives and objects of economic activity are so complex and beautiful that, according to Austrian economist Friedrich Hayek, "all the circumstances which will determine the outcome of a process ... will hardly ever be fully known or measurable."[1]

As a practical matter, this means that economists, like all social scientists, are limited in what they can and cannot know

---

1 Friedrich August von Hayek, "The Pretense of Knowledge," *Nobel Prize Lecture to the Memory of Alfred Nobel*, December 11, 1974, http://www.nobelprize.org/nobel_prizes/economic-sciences/laureates/1974/hayek-lecture.html.

about human behavior. The severe limits on *what* the social scientist can know (epistemology) and *how* he can know it (methodology) is one of Hayek's key insights. While aspects of Hayek's thought ought to be counted among those that Bartholomew says are "troublesome to many Christians," his articulation of the limits of the social sciences is important not only for Christians but also for all people of good will and for that reason should not be dismissed. While it might have seemed strange to him to say this, I think Hayek's insight about the social sciences are a form of intellectual asceticism that (potentially at least) can help put into practice the Patriarch's call to "preserve the mystery of the human person."[2]

Often when people talk about the market, they forget that they are talking about human freedom as it is incarnated economically. Hayek reminds us that if we are not disciplined in our thinking, we easily lapse into deterministic language that overlooks the "great many facts" about the person and the life of the community that "cannot [be] measure[d]." We cannot lose sight of the fact that the social sciences offer us only "very imprecise and general information" about how concrete men and women exercise their freedom.[3]

A good example of this is how the "free" in free market is foremost a negative freedom: It does not tell us anything about what people actually do. Much less does it tell us what people ought to do. Freedom in the market refers *only* to the absence of coercion by a central authority. In a free market, my economic decisions are mine to make. While social pressures and personal circumstance cannot and should not be discounted, relatively speaking no one compels me to make this or that purchase or take one job rather than another. In a market economy, my eco-

---

[2] Patriarch Bartholomew, *Encountering the Mystery: Understanding Orthodox Christianity Today* (New York: Doubleday, 2008), 126.

[3] Hayek, "The Pretense of Knowledge."

nomic decisions are free to the degree that they not mandated by law. However this is a very limited and thin understanding of freedom.

A Robust Economic Freedom

The *Russian Orthodox Church's Basic Teaching on Human Dignity, Freedom and Rights* distinguishes between two types of human freedom. While the "freedom (αὐτεξουσίον [*autexousio*]) of choice" we have in the market is a morally good thing, focusing on it too much can cause us to "ignore the moral dimension of life and the freedom from sin (ἐλευθερία [*eleutheria*])" that is the fruit of divine grace and ascetical struggle. This is why consumerism is an important issue for both economics and moral theology. Consumerism undermines the freedom of the market (*autexousio*) because it undermines the freedom of the person (*eleutheria*). To have a truly free market (to say nothing of a fully human life), we must "be guided by both freedoms." Simply put, "One of these freedoms cannot be defended while the other is neglected. Free adherence to goodness and the truth is impossible without the freedom of choice, just as a free choice loses its value and meaning if it is made in favor of evil."[4]

Returning to our concern here, we can say that consumerism is the pursuit of *freedom of choice* in the economic dimension at the expense of *freedom from evil* in the moral dimension. We need to distinguish consumerism (a sin) from consumption and so from the human being as a consumer.

---

[4] Department of External Church Relations, *The Russian Orthodox Church's Basic Teaching on Human Dignity, Freedom and Rights*, 2.2, available online at https://mospat.ru/en/documents/dignity-freedom-rights/. The original employs bold text here omitted.

Consumption Unredeemed

Economists will often talk of "market failure" or a situation in which the "market on its own fails to produce an efficient allocation of resources." While I do not think this is the intent, there is a decidedly deterministic cast to language like this that suggests our economic life functions without our free participation. This makes a person merely a passive participant in his own economic life rather than a moral actor whose decisions matter.

The economist Enrique Guerra-Pujol argues that legal markets "create incentives for converting mutual conflict into joint cooperation." When these are absent, "illegal or 'black'" markets emerge to fill the void. In addition, one should also expect the level of violence to increase as suppliers compete with each other to corner this lucrative market in the same way in which violent drug cartels fight over the spoils of the illegal drug market. He goes on to identify "three types of legal failure or regulatory impediments to trade. A legal failure occurs (1) when the law fails to define or enforce property rights in a contested resource; (2) when the law criminalizes, prohibits, or otherwise impedes trade in a given good or service; or (3) when the law itself is either uncertain or unclear about what transactions or activities are legal."

He goes on to offer examples of each:

> Textbook examples of the first type of legal failure (lack of well-defined property rights) are common-pool resources such as ocean fisheries, public roads, and waterways. Examples of the second type of legal failure (prohibition), by contrast, are draconian drug laws that make it illegal to buy or sell certain drugs and laws prohibiting prostitution, while a good illustration of the third type of legal failure (legal uncertainty) is the longstanding uncertainty regarding the legality of the purchase and sale of blood. From an economic perspective, such legal uncertainty is

> undesirable because it makes the outcomes of legal cases difficult to predict and hence prevents buyers and sellers from planning their transactions in the shadow of the law or settling their disputes peacefully out of court.[5]

While we may disagree with him regarding how moral or advisable markets for blood or sex are, Guerra-Pujol's observation about legal failure reminds us that personal economic decisions are never purely private. Yes, we are economic actors and not merely passive objects of economic forces. However, we do not act in a social or moral vacuum. Our economic decisions have social implications and are to a degree dependent on cultural factors (like law) that preexist and transcend our personal plans and projects. Again, economic decisions are complex and cannot be reduced either to observable effects or to purely individual intention.

While not an intrinsic part of a market economy, consumerism (as we have discussed it here) represents an example of a third type of failure in the market every bit as important as the two we have just seen. Consumerism embodies a *moral* failure in the market. As a passion, consumerism undermines human freedom and the process of free exchange at the moral and practical foundation of our economic life. This is why we can call consumerism ugly and narcissistic. As we have seen already, like all the passions, consumerism enslaves me to my own desires and alienates me from God and neighbor. This is not poetic or moralizing language but a sober acknowledgment that I can behave in ways that increasingly compromise—and eventually even destroy—my freedom of choice. This means

---

5 Enrique Guerra-Pujol, "Buy or Bite" in *Economics of the Undead: Zombies, Vampires, and the Dismal Science*, ed. Glen Whitman and James Dow (Lanham, MD: Rowman & Littlefield Publishers, 2014), 127.

that while laws and regulations have their place, they cannot solve what is essentially a problem of the heart.

Consumption Redeemed

As we saw earlier, consumption is an essential part of human nature. Though wounded by sin, it nevertheless remains morally good.[6] Moreover, Church historian Helen Rhee reminds us that as bodily creatures "our need to delight in God includes ... enjoy[ing] his creation and abundance through material means.... God's shalom, wholeness, is all-encompassing—material as well as spiritual." This does not mean we are exempt from caring for those in need. It does, however, mean that the poor also have the right to "material things" that, "when properly enjoyed, serve as channels through which God manifests his goodness." For the poor as well as the rich, creation and the human use of creation "are intended to point us toward God, [by] reflecting his beauty, generosity, and glory."[7]

Morally, Rhee continues, this means that consumption "is always conditional in light of God's absolute ownership and creative purpose (the common good)."[8] Far from requiring that human consumption decrease in absolute terms, our pursuit of the common good requires that we expand the circle of those who are able to enjoy the good things of the earth. The poor, too, are called to an enjoyment of creation that is a sign of God's grace and reflects the fruit of their labor. We do not love the poor by impoverishing the rich. Rather, "meeting basic human

---

6 If consumption were not a good thing, then the reception of Holy Communion would be a sin. But the witness of Scripture is clear: We are called to "taste and see that the Lord is good" (Ps. 34:8).

7 Helen Rhee, *Loving the Poor, Saving the Rich: Wealth, Poverty, and Early Christian Formation* (Grand Rapids: Baker Academic, 2012), 193.

8 Rhee, *Loving the Poor, Saving the Rich*, 193.

needs (others' and our own) in terms of providing real access to means of sustenance should be a fundamental ground and goal of economic and political choices, activities, and system."[9] Taking this seriously means that "the concern to meet others' needs takes priority over accumulation of my surplus assets or displays of my refined tastes in luxury items." As we have seen already, while the moral principle is clear, "it is difficult to define concretely what sufficiency and appropriate enjoyment" of creation "would look like."[10] More difficult still is designing public policies that would foster such an outcome.

Patriarch Bartholomew has pointed out that "Western societies have not really found any more beneficial economic mechanism than the markets to regulate the activities of labor and capital." The reason for this is that the free market "forever seeks new ways of reducing costs and increasing gains."[11] He goes on to say that while "there are many advantages to the phenomenon of globalization, there are also serious negative consequences, such as heightened inequality and increased conflict over social, economic, and political priorities."[12] While in "response to the power of markets, governments have a duty to exercise greater responsibility and vigilance," often "governments fail to exercise this responsibility to monitor the activities of international companies and ensure that their productive power is not abused." This does not necessarily reflect moral failure on the part of either governments or business. It is a sober acknowledgement that "[c]ompanies are better at making cross-border connections than [are] regulators or nongovernmental organizations." For this reason, "religious institutions and other independent agencies have a particular obligation to

---

9 Rhee, *Loving the Poor, Saving the Rich*, 193.

10 Rhee, *Loving the Poor, Saving the Rich*, 194.

11 Bartholomew, *Encountering the Mystery*, 170.

12 Bartholomew, *Encountering the Mystery*, 171.

speak out wherever they see that unrestrained globalization is having negative consequences."[13]

In response to the limitations of government, he continues, "religious institutions must insist on the priority of human rights and of social justice, both of which are deeply rooted in civil society and inspired by the faith communities." This means that "[t]ogether with nongovernmental organizations, religious institutions should stand in opposition to trends that favor the concentration of global economic power in the hands of a small number of economically powerful institutions or politically powerful dictators."[14] One value of the free market (and a secular, democratic society) is that it allows the Church the latitude to pursue precisely such an agenda.

Given the complexity of the ethical and practical problems inherent in consumerism, moral suasion is preferable to the exercise of centralized political power. While both can certainly be corrupted to serve self-aggrandizing goals, even under ideal conditions the latter tends to be abstract and so particularly vulnerable to what Hayek called "the inherent limitations of our numerical knowledge which are so often overlooked," even

---

[13] Bartholomew, *Encountering the Mystery*, 171. The economist Donald J. Boudreaux lists several reasons why "even when the problems are genuine and the proposed means of addressing the problems can in principle succeed," governments will often fail "to live up even to the lower standards of performance that most people expect of free markets." Donald J. Boudreaux, "Why Government Fails and Why Ideas Matter," http://www.cato.org/policy-report/novemberdecember-2014/why-governments-fail-why-ideas-matter. For a patristic take on the question see St. Augustine, *The City of God*, 5.4, where he argues that without justice, political authority does not do away with "covetousness" so much as it confers "impunity" on those who in different circumstance we would call pirates or robbers.

[14] Bartholomew, *Encountering the Mystery*, 171.

when (and sometimes especially when) we are pursuing noble and praiseworthy goals.[15]

The Church's witness in this area must begin with the sober acknowledgment that consumerism among the faithful—laity and clergy—is a problem not because we live in a free market but in spite of this. Christians have the freedom of choice (*autexousio*) to make economic decisions that foster a real and substantial freedom from sin (*eleutheria*). While it is comforting to blame materialism or Western culture or capitalism, we are not compelled to make the world's agenda our own. From the beginning, Christians have had to live in the tension of being in the world but not of it (cf. John 17:14–18).

Consumerism is really nothing more or less than human consumption unredeemed by Christ. Consumerism is consumption that conforms to the standards of this world rather than those of Christ. Consumerism is consumption that has not yet been "transformed" ascetically and has not yet been made "good and acceptable" according to the "perfect will of God" (Rom. 12:2). Such transformation requires first a more sophisticated preaching and catechesis on asceticism.[16]

But ascetical purification is not enough.

Where Do We Go from Here?

If, as I have suggested here, consumerism is consumption misdirected, then our production is likewise misdirected. I do not mean that we should cease to create wealth. Economic development is essential if we are to bring the poorest of the poor (to say nothing of the not-so-poor) into the morally right enjoyment of creation.

---

15 Hayek, "The Pretense of Knowledge."

16 For an example of this see, Rhee, *Loving the Poor, Saving the Rich*, 191–220.

In part, this means an expansion of philanthropy. Orthodox ministries such as International Orthodox Christian Charities and FOCUS North American do good work in this area, and they deserve our financial and personal support. True freedom, as Dylan Pahman reminds us, is realized "in serving the needs of others in love" and not simply our own morally legitimate self-interest.[17] What is not always clear—and what I have tried to make at least a bit clearer here—is that when the free market is functioning as it ought to (both morally and economically) this is exactly what happens: self-interest and love of neighbor converge. Building on our philanthropic tradition, we need to look at some of the practical details of economic life. I alluded to one such area earlier: property rights.

Let me add to this another observation from Patriarch Bartholomew. As we have done here, he affirms not only the utilitarian basis of a market economy but also reminds us that the market itself is based on something at once more foundational and broader than mere efficiency:

> [N]ot even the strongest advocates of capitalism would claim that it can serve as a basis for human society unless its activity is underpinned and regulated in the light of moral and spiritual values, which recognize the ultimate value of human beings. Far too often, unrestrained and unregulated markets have led to poverty and pollution. They have failed to curb unemployment and inequality or to protect noneconomic goods, such as culture and ethnic particularity.[18]

---

[17] Dylan Pahman, "The Value of Ordered Liberty: The Orthodox View," *The City* (Summer 2014): 58.

[18] Bartholomew, *Encountering the Mystery*, 170. Advocates for a free market cannot claim, on the one hand, that the market is responsible for myriad improvements in human life without acknowledging as well the human and environmental costs associated with them.

Translating this into effective action requires that Orthodox Christians articulate an appreciative vision of business and entrepreneurship as part of the Christian vocation to "[g]o into all the world and preach the gospel to every creature" (Mark 16:15). This means a true partnership between the bishops as pastors of the Church with lay professionals and business owners so that together they can learn how to create wealth and expand opportunities to the poor in ways that are consonant with holy tradition.[19]

The starting point and goal of this work should, I would suggest, be taken from the apolotikion for the Sunday of Orthodoxy:

> We venerate your most pure icon, loving Lord, as we ask pardon for our offences, Christ God. For by your own choice you were well pleased to ascend the Cross in the flesh, to deliver from the slavery of the enemy those whom you had fashioned. Therefore with thanksgiving we cry to you: you have filled all things with joy, our Saviour, by coming to save the world.[20]

This does not mean that the free market is a morally bad thing, only that—like everything in this life—it is limited and prone to the corrupting influence of sin.

19 Protestant and Roman Catholic scholars as well as popular authors have written extensively on the human vocation to work and its implications for our life in Christ. One of the best is The Pontifical Council for Justice and Peace, *Vocation of the Business Leader: A Reflection*, http://www.pcgp.it/dati/2012-05/04-999999/Vocation%20ENG2.pdf. Only thirty pages long, it would serve as a useful resource for a conversation between business leaders and clergy.

20 "Service of Preparation for the Divine Liturgy," http://www.anastasis.org.uk/Proskom02+notes+diag.pdf.

This hymn captures the central themes we have explored here: ascetical sacrifice and joy as foundational to the Christian life, including our economic life.

The key element, however, is neither ascetical struggle nor sacrifice—essential though they are—but joy. Asceticism and sacrifice, though often hard, ought to be the source of joy. This is true not only spiritually and morally but also economically and materially. Articulating and preaching this joy is, I humbly suggest, the best antidote to consumerism.

Finally, looking back on some of the things I have said as a young priest about economics and business, before I had done any of the research that led to this book, I am quite frankly embarrassed at my ignorance and of the proud and foolish things that I said. For this and more I must ask forgiveness.

Glory to God for all things!

About the Author

Fr. Gregory Jensen is an Orthodox priest and a graduate of the University of Dallas. He earned his PhD from Duquesne University's Institute of Formative Spirituality, an interdisciplinary program in religion, personality theory, and ministry. He has served a mission in rural northern California and ministered to parishes in transition in several states. Currently, he is the Orthodox chaplain at the University of Wisconsin-Madison. In 2013 he was a Loan Mountain Fellow with the Property and Environmental Research Center (PERC) in Bozeman, MT. He has been a long-time contributor to the Acton Institute. In addition to pastoral work, he has led retreats and has been a spiritual director for Orthodox, Catholic, Evangelical, and other Protestant Christians. His published research focuses on personality theory, Christian spirituality, and economics.

22110176R00089

Made in the USA
Middletown, DE
21 July 2015